A Way with Words

A Way with Words

Style in the Age of Artificial Intelligence

John Marsh

University of Michigan Press
Ann Arbor

Published in the United States of America by the
University of Michigan Press

ISBN 978-0-472-04007-0 (print)
ISBN 978-0-472-22243-8 (e-book)

First published January 2026

Authorized Representative: Easy Access System Europe, Mustamäe tee 50, 10621 Tallinn, Estonia, gpsr.requests@easproject.com

Contents

Acknowledgments

It takes many hands to bring a book into the world. Thanks to LeAnn Fields, Katie LaPlant, Haley Winkle, Juliette Snyder, and Danielle Coty-Fattal at the University of Michigan Press. Thanks to the anonymous readers of the manuscript, one of whom pushed me to think about what a contemporary style guide could do. And thanks to Jessica Klimoff for help with the final preparation of the manuscript.

Preface

I wrote this book because I could not find another like it.

A Way with Words aims to help writers with the essentials of style. By style, I do not mean grammar, although style occasionally includes grammar. Rather, I mean writing clear, concise, and lively prose: eliminating wordiness, using active verbs, avoiding run-on sentences. These are the issues, and not when to use *who* or *whom*, that most often bedevil student writers. And these are the issues that will stand out to their teachers, employers, and clients.

While composing this book, I have kept in mind why writers should buy it—or, in the case of students, be made to buy it—when they could consult online (and free) websites like the Purdue Owl. The answer is that while those sites cost nothing, they end up costing a lot. To begin with, they are chaotically organized. In the chaos, they flatten out what matters more and what matters less. Crucial lessons on concision sit side by side with cryptic lessons on separable phrasal verbs. This method of organization is fine if you know what you don't know. But if you don't know what you don't know, where do you start? The arrangement also ensures that lessons exist in siloes, each occurring independently of the other. That makes it difficult if not impossible for writers who hope to put it all together. Worse, these guides sometimes offer bad advice. For example, writers have more strategies for handling clichés than simply eliminating them.

Perhaps worst of all, the entries on these sites are joyless. They read like they were written by no one and for no one. They confirm what everyone already suspects, which is that discussions of writing in general and style in particular are as dull as dishwater.

In what follows, I say little about style that has not been said before, but I have tried to correct for these flaws. Instead of trying to cover every topic,

I cover only the most essential ones. In terms of organization, I put first things first. In other words, I organize the book by how urgently I would like to correct a given style issue in a piece of student writing. While reading a first set of papers, for example, I almost immediately want to start drawing lines through words to hack away at the wordiness. I have learned, therefore, that before students turn in a first paper, I need to devote lessons to concision and the passive voice. Later on, I can teach them to scrub pretentious diction from their vocabulary or to vary the length of their sentences. Some instructors may have different priorities, but I think mine are fairly representative and, if not, teachers can choose in which order to assign the chapters. Readers without teachers can choose in which order to read them.

To combat the silo effect, at the end of the book I include paragraphs that mix and match issues (vague pronouns, sentence fragments, punctuating quotations) from previous chapters and ask writers to edit the entire passage.

And to ward off the joylessness, I try to hold a conversation instead of giving a lecture. In addition, and unlike most style guides written for students, which provide sample sentences from what seems like a stunningly insipid world, I draw examples from essays that students might actually write. As for cost, I cannot compete with free, but I have tried to keep the price low by not tacking on sections devoted to research practices, different citation styles (APA, MLA, Chicago), or that venerable method of padding out writing guides, a list of commonly confused words.

Throughout this book, I urge writers to think about who will read what they write, and why their readers should listen to what they have to say. Here let me take my own advice.

Whom do I write for? I am a teacher, so this book is drawn from lessons I offer my students every semester. Since I teach in the humanities, what I say mostly applies to writers in those disciplines. For example, I urge writers to use the active rather than the passive voice. (*Thomas Paine wrote* Common Sense versus Common Sense *was written by Thomas Paine.*) In the sciences, by contrast, writers can and do use the passive voice. (*We titrated the acid solution* versus *The acid solution was titrated.*) That is not to say, however, that I have written the book exclusively for students in the humanities. Most of the advice I give—provide transitions, vary sentence length, use plain language—applies to writing regardless of the field. It also applies to writing regardless of the context. In other words, I do not teach students these lessons so that they can impress me, their instructor. I teach them so that they can take them with them to other classes and other rhetorical situations, including their eventual workplaces. In short, good writing is good writing, and it is welcome everywhere.

Readers may also wonder why they should listen to me. I am a writer, of course, so I have spent a lifetime learning and practicing these fundamentals. But more to the point, I am a teacher. I estimate that I have taught 1,800 students and graded 5,600 essays over the last twenty-five years. (By the time you read this preface, the numbers will be higher.) I would like to think that all of those years, all of those students, and all of those essays have taught me what good writing looks like. I would also like to think that they have taught me how to help those who want to improve their writing.

In the book, I address two subjects that I want to flag here. The first is the argument that standards of style like the ones I recommend in this book may discriminate against other ways of using language. The obvious though insufficient response to this objection is that so long as these standards exist, every student needs to know them; if not, they will be at a disadvantage to other students in the classroom and, eventually, to other writers in the workplace. Yet I think the standards have a more fundamental purpose than simply dressing the part. I expand on this discussion in the introduction and in the chapter on inclusion.

The second subject is that, as I discuss in the introduction, artificial intelligence programs like ChatGPT and Gemini are changing how we think about and practice (or not) the craft of writing. No one can know exactly what these changes will bring. But *A Way with Words* invites readers to think about what is changing and how they can respond to it. It offers advice about how writers can distinguish their writing from the assembly-line prose artificial intelligence tends to generate, and what they stand to gain from doing so.

I enjoyed writing this book. I hope writers find it enjoyable—and useful—to read.

Introduction

Everyone knows about synonyms and antonyms. A synonym is a word that means roughly the same thing as another word. For example, *quick* and *fast*. An antonym is a word that means the opposite of another word, like *light* and *dark*. Fewer people know about contronyms. A contronym is one of those rare words that can mean one thing and its exact opposite. Put differently, it is a word that is its own antonym.

Take a word like *cleave*. It can mean to sever something. *With my axe, I cleaved the branches from the tree.* It can also mean to adhere to something (or someone). *Scared for their lives, the shipwrecked crew cleaved to each other in the water.*

Like *cleave*, *style* is a contronym. On the one hand, newspapers like *The New York Times* and presses like the University of Chicago have so-called style manuals. These guides ensure that everyone who writes for a given publisher follows the same set of rules. For example, is it the Titanic or the *Titanic*? Since arguments can be made for both conventions, style manuals designate which one writers should adopt. (*The New York Times* says the Titanic. *The Chicago Manual of Style* prefers the *Titanic*.) These conventions are often referred to as house styles. In other words, when you are in this house, you will follow these rules. In this usage, *style* means uniformity.

On the other—and opposite—hand, *style* means that which makes something (or someone) original or unique. Figure skaters, for example, are rated for the technical elements of their performance. Each maneuver—an Axel jump, a Biellmann spin—has a starting value that rises or falls according to how well the skater executes it. But figure skaters are also rated on the artistic elements of their performance. That means two skaters could perform the identical program and execute it equally well, but one skater may outscore the other because of some indefinite quality they bring to the routine. How well does the skater embody the music they select? Does the skater use facial expressions and body language to convey the emotion of a performance? Does the skater connect with spectators and draw them into the performance? Another word for these indefinite qualities is style. In this usage, *style* is the opposite of uniformity. Instead, it means individuality.

This is a book about style in writing. Which definition of the word do I mean? Uniformity or individuality? The short answer is both.

Character and Clarity

Although style guides occasionally differ over the finer points—the Titanic versus the *Titanic*—they agree about almost everything else. Use the active voice. Avoid clichés. Watch out for fragments and run-on sentences. Choose plain words over fancy ones. Italicize the titles of books (*Leaves of Grass*) but set items within those books between quotation marks ("Song of Myself"). If a parenthesis comes at the end of a sentence, place the period outside it. And so on. This book outlines these expectations and gives students a chance to practice them so that they can compose or revise their writing accordingly.

I discuss the other definition of style below, but when it comes to the uniformity of style, why should you, the writer, care about following these guidelines? For a couple of reasons, each of which has to do with the relationship between you and your reader.

The first reason is *ethos*, a word that derives from the ancient Greek word for *character*. Those who read what you write want to feel like they are in safe hands. They will ask, does this writer care enough about writing to write well? Do they follow the conventions of writing? Or do they cut corners? Write slapdash sentences? Invent their own rules for punctuation? In sum, readers want to know if they can trust your character as a writer. If so, they will be more likely to listen to what you have to say. If not, they may not even give you a hearing.

The second reason to care about following rules like use the active voice or avoid clichés also has to do with readers, but this reason can seem more concrete than how readers judge your character as a writer. This second reason has to do with the experience of reading itself. Do readers feel like the writer makes it easy to understand what they say? Or do readers feel like they have to struggle to grasp what a writer means? For example, in chapter four of this book, I discuss vague pronouns. Consider these two sentences:

> Van Gogh's fascination with the interplay of light and color, exemplified in works such as *Starry Night,* demonstrated his technical virtuosity but also his profound spiritual and philosophical beliefs. This imbued his art with a transcendent quality that continues to captivate viewers and influence artists to this day.

What does the *This* that begins the second sentence refer to? Does it mean Van Gogh's fascination with the interplay of light and color? His technical virtuosity? His profound spiritual and philosophical beliefs? All three? The writer needs to say which. If not, the reader has to do the work the writer should have done for them, and they may never arrive at the right answer regardless of the work they put in. That carelessness will chip away at the ethos of the writer. Why should I trust this writer when they leave me to do their work? But the ambiguity of the word *This* also chips away at what the writer, regardless of the character they project, hopes to communicate to readers. In other words, the vagueness of the *This* endangers clarity.

Both of these reasons—call them character and clarity—exemplify the first definition of style. Uniformity gets a bad name in a culture that prizes individuality. But readers expect writers to meet certain standards, even if following those standards seems like it might lead to standardization. I say *seems* because in reality standards do not always result in standardization.

Voice

Most discussions of style end here. Here are the rules. Follow them. If you do not, you will lose your readers, either because they do not trust you or because they do not understand you. But following the rules serves another purpose. If you respect the conventions of writing, you can open the door to the second definition of style, that of individuality.

Some writers achieve individuality by breaking all the rules. (The novelist James Joyce comes to mind.) But the second sense of style does not usually come from breaking rules. Rather, it comes from working within the rules to establish your voice as a writer. Just as no two figure skaters will give identical performances, even if their arrangement of jumps and spins is identical, no two writers will sound the same. Nor should they. Your job as a writer includes bringing what makes you unique—your experience, your interpretation of the world, your voice—to your writing. You may not think you have a voice, something that sets your writing apart from others, but you do. However, it will not find you. You have to find it. If you can bring this voice to your writing, readers will keep reading not just because you earn their trust or clearly state what you mean. They will keep reading because they like spending time with you, like listening to what you and you alone have to say. To speak paradoxically, if you take care of style, if you follow the rules, you can cultivate your own style.

Why Bother?

At this point, you might be thinking why go to the trouble of writing when I can have someone—or something—write for me. I speak, of course, of artificial intelligence. The sentences above about Vincent Van Gogh were generated by ChatGPT 3.5, the most commonly used version (as of this writing) of the software that allows users to prompt a chatbot to do any number of things, including writing just about anything you ask it to write. ChatGPT and other large language model systems work by scraping the hundreds of billions of gigabytes of data from the internet and using that content to answer a question or respond to a command. The program interprets what a user inputs, generates a provisional answer to that input, and then, working from its database of extant sentences on the internet, predicts which word most likely follows another word until it has assembled a response. The output, which in this case is a piece of writing, can seem almost human.

All of which leads to a question. If ChatGPT can create such passable prose, why should students—why should anyone—go to the trouble of writing anything themselves? If I need to divide one number by another, I do not sit down at a table with a pencil and a piece of paper to do long division by hand. I reach for the calculator on my phone, enter the two numbers, and presto. According to this way of thinking, writing is like long division. Why waste the day doing something a computer can do more quickly and, perhaps, more accurately?

If you are enrolled in college, one reason not to do so is because of plagiarism, which, in this context, my university defines as "submitting work created by generative technology without attribution." In other words, do not let ChatGPT do your work for you because you might get caught and suffer the consequences for getting caught. At my university, the consequences range from redoing the assignment to failing the course. An arms race is currently playing out between sophisticated users of artificial intelligence and sophisticated programs designed to identify the work of artificial intelligence. You do not want to get caught on the wrong side of that arms race.

Yet avoiding artificial intelligence out of fears of plagiarism begs the question. It assumes that plagiarism, if that is in fact what happens when we prompt AI to write something for us, is bad. But is it? Why not let ChatGPT compose my essay? According to my university, because doing so is a form of misrepresentation. I pass off work as my own that is not in fact mine. But so what? If writing has a purely instrumental function—the shareholders need this report, the funding agency needs that grant proposal—then who cares who wrote it? Or what wrote it? For example, artificial intelligence can now write competent articles about a professional baseball game. Most baseball fans do not care about the author of the article. They just want to know how the game played out, who won, who performed well, what the game means for the playoff race, and so on. If most of the writing the world needs is like an article about a baseball game, then writing does not have to come from a human. It simply has to say what needs to be said. If you believe this argument, then you will think that eventually universities will realize that asking students to compose their own prose is like asking them to do their own long division.

So, why bother learning about the active voice, clichés, fragments, run-on sentences, plain words, formatting titles, where to put periods, and so on? Instead, simply train an artificial intelligence program to follow these rules, prompt it, and then sit back and watch it spit out what it spits out.

I acknowledge the temptation and the uses of artificial intelligence. Writing is hard. We have other responsibilities and perhaps better uses of our time. But I think artificial intelligence gives students more—not fewer—reasons to care about writing and style.

The first reason comes back to the question of voice. By design, large language model systems like ChatGPT sound like everyone else. In order to predict which word comes next, the program has to consult what millions of other writers have already said. Its voice, therefore, derives from all the voices in its dataset. That makes it, by definition, derivative. On the one hand, derivative is good. Derivative means the prose ChatGPT generates follows most of the style guidelines outlined in this book and, therefore, creates acceptable writing that readers can understand. On the other hand, derivative is bad. The text ChatGPT creates sounds, well, it sounds robotic, which is not surprising since ChatGPT is little more than a sophisticated robot. One of the reasons I can get away with using AI-generated examples in this book without acknowledging copyright is that copyright law, at least in the United States, only covers work written by humans. AI is not human. It merely does a passing imitation of one. True, by feeding it snippets of your own prose, you can train ChatGPT to write like you and not like everyone else. But in my experience, the writing it generates does not sound like me at all. It sounds like a poor imitation of me.

From a writerly perspective, then, derivative is welcome. It leaves room for you to do what ChatGPT cannot do, which is to write prose that sounds like you, that includes and projects your voice. Even ChatGPT knows this about itself and about you. How do I know? I asked it.

> Me: "Will ChatGPT replace human writing?"
>
> Chat GPT: While ChatGPT can generate text based on the input it receives, it lacks the creativity, intuition, and contextual understanding that humans bring to the writing process. Human writers can incorporate personal experiences, emotions, and cultural nuances into their writing in ways that AI cannot replicate. So, while ChatGPT can be a helpful tool, human writing will likely remain an essential and valued skill.

ChatGPT could just be humoring me. If it were going to replace human writing, would it tell me? But if ChatGPT is right that human writing will remain an essential and valued skill, that is because human readers will always prefer good writing with creativity, intuition, and contextual understanding—that is, good writing with a voice—to the lowest common denominator prose that artificial intelligence generates. Think of it this way: good writing that has a voice—your voice—will almost always win out over good-enough writing that does not. Want to impress the professors? The shareholders? The foundation agencies? Write like a human being and not like a large language model artificial intelligence program.

Not Showing but Learning

The second reason to keep your prose in house and not outsource it to ChatGPT or other artificial intelligences is because writing is not always instrumental. By which I mean writing is not always about earning a grade, addressing the shareholders, or securing a grant. The purpose of writing may not be to communicate what you already know. The purpose may be to discover what you think.

In my day job, I teach poetry. I have lost count of how many times I thought I understood a poem only to discover, when I write about it, that

I have missed so much. Similarly, I have an intuition about how I feel about the major political issues of the day (climate change, immigration, income inequality, political polarization), but only after writing about an issue do I arrive at what I truly think about it.

In short, writing is learning. And writers have known about this reason to write for a long time. Many have said a version of the following, but more often than not the novelist E. M. Forster receives the credit: "How do I know what I think until I see what I say?" Diaries and journals give writers a chance to see what they say. Yet there is something about writing for others—for readers—that focuses the mind. We learn what we think not just by seeing what we have to say but by testing what we think against what we imagine our readers will think. And as soon as you write for readers, you have to think about style, about meeting the standards outlined in this book so that you can communicate with readers *and* so you can create a voice that will make them want to read you.

Style Is Not...

A quick word about what style is not. First, it is not grammar. True, you need to know a handful of basic grammatical terms like subject, verb, and object to follow along, but for the most part you can learn about style without falling down the hole of restrictive versus non-restrictive clauses, the subjunctive versus the indicative mood, and so on.

Second, style is not, or it should not be, a way of separating the righteous from the damned. Indeed, some rules of style seem so arbitrary that recommending them, let alone enforcing them, feels more like policing those who do not follow them than it does like making it easier for readers and writers to understand each other. For example, some style guides recommend that writers should only compare like items. That is, instead of writing this:

> The depths of Shakespeare's plays exceeds his sonnets.

One should write this:

> The depths of Shakespeare's plays exceeds **the depths of** his sonnets.

I can see the reason for this rule. In the first sentence, the writer compares "the depths of Shakespeare's plays" to "his sonnets." But we do not want to compare the depths of plays to sonnets per se. We want to compare *the depths* of plays to *the depths* of sonnets. But I doubt many readers trip over what the first sentence means or question the character of the writer who commits the error. In fact, I suspect that many readers would not even notice the inconsistency. In this book, I try to discuss only the things that most readers will notice.

Like *cleave* and *style*, *trim* is also a contronym. On the one hand, it can mean to take away, to remove something. *If you do not trim the ivy, it will take over the yard.* On the other hand, *trim* can mean to decorate, to add something. At Christmas, we speak of trimming the tree (adding ornaments, tinsel, and a star). You can think of *style* the same way you do *trim*. What can you take away from your writing to make it better? And what can you add to your writing to make it better still? Finally, what combination of taking away and adding will allow you to make what you write your own?

This book shows you.

CHAPTER 1

A ~~Difficult~~ Dilemma: On Concision

If you have ever wondered why some nineteenth-century novels are so damn long, consider the incentives for writers and publishers. During that period, novelists like Charles Dickens and Leo Tolstoy often published their work serially. In other words, chapters from their novels would first appear in periodicals and only later as complete novels. *Anna Karenina*, for example, was published from 1875 to 1877 in the monthly magazine *The Russian Messenger*. The arrangement benefited editors. Eager to find out what happened next, readers would snatch up copies of their magazines. Eager to make money, editors wanted to capitalize on readerly interest for as long as possible. Give us more, they told novelists. For their part, novelists had slightly different but nevertheless aligned incentives. Often, they would be paid by the word. The arrangement all but guaranteed long novels. Editors wanted as much content as possible, and writers wanted as much cash as possible. The result? All 864 pages of *Anna Karenina*.

Student writers also have what economists call perverse incentives. By perverse, they do not mean sexually perverse; rather, they mean an incentive that produces unintended or undesirable effects. Unlike nineteenth-century novelists, most student writers do not get paid by the word. But they do need to fill as much space as possible with as little effort as possible. In both cases, the incentive is the same: use as many words as possible.

Consider a student sitting down to write a four-to-six-page paper on educational inequalities. They begin by worrying about how they will ever fill that many pages. So, they think, why use one word when they could use six? Why write *since* when they could write *in light of the fact that*:

> ~~Since~~ **In light of the fact that** students from lower-income households often lack access to quality educational resources and

opportunities, educational inequalities persist and contribute to widening gaps in academic achievement and socioeconomic outcomes.

In light of the fact that gets you five words closer to finishing the essay than does *since*. It also sounds more impressive than plain old *since.* You would be a fool not to use it.

Unless, of course, using *in light of the fact that* instead of *since* makes you look like a fool. And it does. It commits one of the great sins of writing: wordiness.

In this chapter (on phrases) and in the next two (on sentences), you will learn why you should write concisely and how to do so. I should warn you, though, that writing concisely is not something you learn how to do all at once. It has to become a habit, and like most habits, it takes time and effort to develop. But it is time and effort well spent. Learning how to write concisely is one of the best things a writer can do to improve their prose.

In many chapters of this book, I depart from the conventional writing wisdom. Avoid clichés like the plague? Well, maybe one or two is OK. Eschew fancy words? Sure, most of the time, but why not indulge in one from time to time? In this chapter, however, the conventional wisdom is spot on. Everyone, or nearly everyone, agrees that writing concisely, like brushing your teeth, is a virtuous habit to cultivate. Not everyone, however, agrees on how to do it.

The first and most important lesson is to rid yourself of the belief that the more words you use—and thus the more space in an essay you quickly and effortlessly fill—the better. You are not Leo Tolstoy. Instead of being paid by the word, imagine that you have to pay for every word you use. Treat words as scarce resources. Do not waste them. And recognize that readers would rather have four pages of tight prose than six pages of windiness.

~~Prior to~~ Before

I have said that wordiness comes in one of two forms: the phrase and the sentence. However, the category of the phrase divides into two subcategories: wordy phrases and redundant phrases. *In light of the fact that* is a wordy phrase. You can substitute *since* without losing anything. By contrast, a phrase like *collaborate together* is redundant. If two or more people *collaborate*, to say they collaborate *together* is silly. *Collaborate* means to work together. You can drop *together.*

In the first category, wordy phrases, you can substitute a word for a phrase, just as we did when we substituted *since* for *in light of the fact that.* Take this sentence:

> The study predicted that individuals with high levels of social support would exhibit lower levels of depressive symptoms on the grounds that social support buffers against stress.

For *on the grounds that,* you can substitute *because*:

> The study predicted that individuals with high levels of social support would exhibit lower levels of depressive symptoms ~~on the grounds that~~ **because** social support buffers against stress.

In sentences like these, single words like *since, because, must,* or *should* can stand in for phrases composed of three, four, or five words.

With redundant phrases, however, the strategy is not substitution but deletion. See if you can spot the redundant phrase in this sentence:

> To effectively regulate artificial intelligence, policymakers must plan ahead to anticipate and mitigate potential risks and ethical dilemmas.

To plan is to plan ahead. You cannot plan behind. You do not need *ahead*:

> To effectively regulate artificial intelligence, policymakers must plan ~~ahead~~ to anticipate and mitigate potential risks and ethical dilemmas.

If wordy phrases invite friendly substitution, redundant phrases require cold-blooded deletion.

In *Style: Toward Clarity and Grace,* Joseph Williams offers a list of forty or so wordy phrases and the single words that can substitute for them. Similarly, web sites will list the "50 Redundant Phrases to Avoid." These lists are useful, but you have to memorize them if you hope to spot instances in your own writing. That asks a lot. I struggle to remember the four or five things I need from the grocery store. My chances of remembering forty or fifty phrases—twice that if we count both wordy and redundant phrases—are nil.

So, in this chapter, I try a different approach. Instead of asking you to memorize innumerable phrases, I give you ten of the more common examples from each category. I have two hopes for this approach.

First, that by memorizing the most common wordy or redundant phrases, you can get more bang for your buck. The redundant phrase *end result*, for example, does not constitute two percent of all instances of redundant phrases. (One divided by fifty.) *End result*—it should just be *result*, by the way—appears more often than almost any other redundant phrase. Compare the relatively rare but no less dreadful *foreign imports*. (If *import* means to bring something into a country to sell it, which it does, then everything imported is necessarily foreign.) According to Google Books Ngram Viewer, the phrase *end result* is seventy-eight times as common as *foreign imports*. If you can turn *end result* into *result*, you will have got a good start on jettisoning the redundant phrases that weigh down your prose.

Second, I hope that by memorizing the more common examples of wordy and redundant phrases, you will understand the logic of each and will be able to apply that reasoning to other instances. In other words, by focusing on the most common wordy or redundant phrases, you can more easily spot other ones in your writing. If so, then the virtue of concision will depend on mindset as much as it does on memory.

In that spirit, here are some of the more common wordy phrases and their one-word substitutes:

1. **A majority of** = *most*
   ~~A majority of~~ **Most** participants reported feeling a substantial decrease in stress levels after engaging in mindfulness meditation practices.

2. **A number of** = *some*, *several*, or *many*
   ~~A number of~~ **Many** studies have shown that social inequality and economic disparity contribute significantly to community health disparities and access to educational opportunities.

3. **At this point in time** = *now*, *currently*, or just delete it
   ~~At this point in time, the~~ **The** national economy is experiencing significant growth, driven by increased consumer spending and robust investment in the technology sector.

4. **Because of the fact that** or **Due to the fact that** or **In light of the fact that** or **In view of the fact that** or **On account of the fact that** = *because* or *since*
~~On account of the fact that~~ **Because** the novel is set during a time of political turmoil, the author uses the protagonist's journey as a metaphor for the larger societal changes happening around him.

5. **Despite the fact that** or **In spite of the fact that** = *although*
~~Despite the fact that~~ **Although** existentialism often emphasizes individual freedom and choice, it also acknowledges the inherent responsibilities and anxieties that come with this freedom.

6. **Has the ability to** or **Has the opportunity to** = *can*
In this study, we investigate how word order in Mandarin Chinese ~~has the ability to~~ **can** convey subtle nuances of meaning.

7. **In the event that** = *if*
~~In the event that~~ **If** sales projections are not met, the company has contingency plans in place to adjust marketing strategies and cut costs to maintain profitability.

8. **With the exception of** = *except for*
~~With the exception of~~ **Except for** the Industrial Revolution, few periods have had as profound an impact on economic and social structures as the Renaissance.

9. **It is important that** or **It is necessary that** or **It is crucial that** or **It is essential that** = *must* or *should*
~~It is important that~~ [P]olicymakers **should** consider the long-term effects of inflation on economic stability.

10. **It is possible that** = *may, might, can,* or *could*
~~It is possible that~~ [T]he ambiguity in the character's motives **may** add to the richness of the narrative, allowing for diverse interpretations.

Note that in some instances—see *It is important that* and *It is possible that*—you cannot simply substitute one word for a wordy phrase. Sometimes you have to modify the sentence to make room for the better, more concise word. Regardless, if we are paying by the word instead of being paid by the word, replacing wordy phrases with their one-word equivalent lowers our bill considerably.

~~Needlessly~~ Redundant

I enjoy swapping one word for a wordy phrase. But nothing compares to the thrill of lopping off the heads of redundant phrases. Here are some of the most common redundant phrases and which words to cut:

1. **Ask a question**
   Sometimes you need to specify what you or someone is asking:

   > In the poem's closing lines, the poet uses vivid imagery to ask a question that lingers in the reader's mind, inviting deeper reflection on the human condition.

   But since *ask* implies to ask a question, you can often do away with *a question*:

   > The protagonist's inner conflict allows the author to ask ~~a question~~ about the nature of sacrifice and its impact on personal growth.

2. **At the present time**
   Present is already a time. It is the time now occurring. Therefore, *at the present time* is redundant. *At present* will do. You could also just write *currently* or nothing at all. Let the present tense verb do its job:

   > ~~At the present time, there~~ **There** is a lack of consensus among researchers regarding the efficacy of this particular therapeutic approach.

   See also *oftentimes*. *Often* is already a measure of time. It would make no more sense to say *oftentimes* than it would to say *large in size*. *Large* is already a size. Cut *times*:

   > In economic theory, market equilibrium is often~~times~~ disrupted by unforeseen events such as natural disasters or political unrest.

The phrase *At this point in time* suffers from the same problem. A point in time is already a time. If you mean *At this point in time* to refer to a moment in the past, just say *Then*:

> ~~At this point in time,~~ Rome was **then** at the height of its power.

3. **Consensus of opinion**
Consensus already implies opinions. Opinions are what everyone in the consensus agrees to. Perhaps judges could have a consensus of opinions, because opinions are what they write. For everyone one else, just drop *opinion*:

> The consensus ~~of opinion~~ among contemporary philosophers is that the mind-body problem remains one of the most challenging issues in the field of metaphysics.

4. **Concept of**
Instead of saying *the concept of* something, you can usually just say the thing:

> ~~The concept of moral~~ Moral relativism challenges the idea of universal ethical standards.

5. **End result**
A *result* is the outcome of something. If so, then just as most outcomes are final outcomes, so most *results* are final results. You can cut *end*:

> The ~~end~~ result of the policy change was a noticeable shift in societal attitudes toward mental health issues.

I can imagine times when *end result* may be appropriate. If you are speaking of different and intermediate results of something, you might well want to say *end result*. But that very rarely happens.

6. **First began**
If something *began* (started, opened, appeared) it must have *first* began. Could it have *second* began? Cut *first*:

> The movement for civil rights ~~first~~ began as a grassroots effort in response to systemic racial discrimination.

So too *Past history*. History always occurs in the past. You can lose *past*:

> To fully grasp the cultural significance of a ritual, anthropologists must delve into the ~~past~~ history of the community practicing it.

See also *past memories* and *future plans.*

7. **It is evident that**

   If something is true, it is already evident that it is true. You do not need to speak of evidence. Strike the whole phrase:

   > ~~It is evident that the~~ The exploitation of natural resources without regard for ecological balance leads to long-term environmental degradation.

8. **Possible alternatives**

   By definition, *alternatives* present *possibilities.* Cut it:

   > When addressing climate change, policymakers must examine ~~possible~~ alternatives to fossil fuels, such as renewable energy sources and advanced nuclear technology.

   See also *various differences.*

9. **Serves to**

   If something does something, it will almost always serve to do something else. Strike *serves to*:

   > The introduction of strict regulations ~~serves to protect~~ **protects** consumers from fraudulent practices.

10. **Still remains**

    Something that *remains* is still in place. You do not need *still*:

    > Even with advancements in technology and policing strategies, the issue of repeat offenders in our society ~~still~~ remains.

Finally, I cannot pass over one more redundant phrase: *the way in which.* There is also a plural version: *the ways in which.* I used to only hear (or read) *the way in which* from academics, but like an invasive species, it has begun to colonize other domains of writing. Indeed, the phrase has now become a verbal tic:

> Gender identity is a deeply personal aspect of self-discovery, and *the ways in which* individuals express their gender can vary widely.

One loses nothing, except the pretense of profundity, by simply deleting *in which*:

> Gender identity is a deeply personal aspect of self-discovery, and the ways ~~in which~~ individuals express their gender can vary widely.

Or you can just substitute *how*:

> Gender identity is a deeply personal aspect of self-discovery, and ~~the ways in which~~ **how** individuals express their gender can vary widely.

I wish I could put into words the ways ~~in which~~ the phrase *the ways in which* grate on my tender soul.

Paired Words

If a redundant phrase uses two words when one would do, then the following sentence is redundant but in a slightly different way than we have seen so far:

> The study explores the inequality and disparity in access to healthcare among different socioeconomic groups, highlighting systemic issues within the healthcare system.

Here the problem is not a wordy phrase like *despite the fact that* or *it is important that*. Nor is it quite the same problem as a redundant phrase like *at the present time* or *unexpected surprise*. Instead, the problem is that the writer refuses to choose between two synonyms: *inequality* and *disparity*.

If you are a cynic, you could say that by including both *inequality* and *disparity*, the writer is trying to fill space, as when someone writes *at the same time as* instead of just *as*. More generously, you could say that the writer is not quite sure whether they mean *inequality* or *disparity*, so they try both on for size. No two words are perfectly alike. If they were, we would not have two words but one. Nevertheless, the words resemble each other enough that when they appear next to each other, a reader will wonder why the writer did not choose one over the other. Does the writer mean inequality? Or does the writer mean disparity? In the moment, the writer may not know, but eventually they have to return to the sentence and decide which one suits. In other words, they have to choose one:

> The study explores the ~~inequality and~~ disparity in access to healthcare among different socioeconomic groups, highlighting systemic issues within the healthcare system.

Of the two species of verbosity, wordy phrases and redundant ones, what I am calling paired words more closely resembles redundant phrases. As with a phrase like *still remains*, the writer is not called upon to substitute one word for a longer phrase but to toss ~~or heave~~ one word overboard altogether.

Postscript: That

Speaking of tossing words overboard, almost everyone agrees that you can sometimes do away with the word *that* in a sentence. The debate is about how often you can do away with it. At minimum, most think you do not need *that* after the verb *say* or *think*:

> One of the central questions in epistemology is whether we can truly say ~~that~~ we know something if our justification for that belief is based on unreliable or incomplete information.

Or:

> In ethical theory, consequentialists think ~~that~~ the moral worth of an action is determined by its outcomes, while deontologists argue that certain actions are inherently right or wrong, irrespective of their consequences.

Others want to add other *that*-less verbs to the list: *know*, *claim*, *hear*, *believe*.

> In moral philosophy, some philosophers believe ~~that~~ ethical principles are objective and universal, while others argue for a more relativistic approach based on cultural or individual beliefs.

Still others want to include nouns that express *possibility* or *feeling* as occasions to delete *that*:

> In discussions of free will and determinism, philosophers often consider whether it is possible ~~that~~ human actions are predetermined by factors such as genetics and environment, or if individuals have genuine freedom to choose their actions.

And an ambitious few will want to expand the campaign against *that* to adjectives like *sad* or *glad*:

> In his existentialist writings, Jean-Paul Sartre expresses a radical freedom where individuals are glad ~~that~~ they are responsible for creating their own essence through their choices.

As a rule, I stop at verbs (*say*, *think*, *know*, *claim*, *hear*, *believe*) but spare the *that* following nouns and adjectives. Or I will just trust my ear. Does the sentence sound fine without its *that*? Nix it. Does it sound off without it? Then keep it.

So What?

At this point, I can hear some readers muttering, so what? Say I prune my prose of wordy phrases like *due to the fact that* (instead of *because*) and redundant phrases like *absolutely certain* (instead of just *certain*). What have I gained? In the first instance, I save four words. In the second, one word. Who cares? Especially if, as this chapter implies, many writers, maybe a majority of them, also deal in wordy and redundant phrases. Those writers, who are also readers, may not even notice the wordiness.

As with so many of the other guidelines in this book, the answer to the question—so what? who cares?—is you. You should care. Although a majority of readers will neither notice nor object to the *absolutely* in *absolutely certain*, some readers will. And those readers matter. Since writing is thinking, they may conclude that a careless writer means a careless thinker. To put it frankly, when those readers come across a phrase like *due to the fact that*, they may suspect the writer of filling up the time while waiting for a boat, as the great American poet Walt Whitman put it. Needless to say, you do not want them to think that of you or your writing.

The other response to the question ("Who cares?") is aesthetic. Michelangelo famously said that "the sculpture is already complete within the marble block, before I start my work. It is already there, I just have to chisel away the superfluous material." You can think of a piece of writing as a sculpture. Instead of a marble block, you have a draft. And, like Michelangelo, you have to chisel away the superfluous material, the wordy and redundant phrases, to liberate its inner *David.* All of that is to say phrases like *due to the fact that* and *absolutely certain* mar your prose as much as random lumps of marble would mar *David.* If only for its own sake, you should want what you write to be as clean and tight as possible.

Anna Karenina is a great book, one of my favorites. But it is not the best model for most writers.

Exercises

1. Below are some sentences containing wordy phrases. Some of them you have seen in this chapter, and others you have not. Substitute one word for the whole phrase. If you struggle, here are some words that might help: *although, because, can, concerning, if, might, must, since, some, soon.*
   A. An artist who has the opportunity to study under a master painter gains not only technical skills but also a deep understanding of the artistic traditions and techniques passed down through generations.
   B. In the near future, further research into the artist's lesser-known sketches may provide deeper insights into their evolving creative process.
   C. Considering the fact that the Renaissance period marked a significant revival of interest in classical art and learning, it is not surprising that many artists of the time sought to emulate the styles and techniques of ancient Greek and Roman art.
   D. It is crucial that art historians carefully examine the brushstrokes and color palette of the painting to determine the artist's stylistic influences and the historical context in which it was created.
   E. It is possible that the shift in the artist's color palette during this period reflects a deeper emotional or philosophical evolution in his work.
   F. In light of the fact that the artist was deeply influenced by the Romantic movement, his paintings often depict dramatic landscapes with a sense of sublime beauty and awe-inspiring nature.

G. In reference to the artist's use of light and shadow, scholars have noted a similarity between his techniques and those employed by Baroque painters to create a sense of depth and drama in their compositions.
H. In spite of the fact that the artist faced criticism for his unconventional techniques, his paintings are now celebrated for their innovative approach to color and form.
I. In the event that new evidence comes to light regarding the provenance of the painting, art historians may need to reassess its attribution to determine its true origins.
J. A number of Renaissance artists, such as Leonardo da Vinci and Michelangelo, revolutionized the art world with their innovative techniques and profound artistic vision.

2. Below is a list of nouns, verbs, and adjectives. Look up their definition, then take or adapt one word from the definition to create your own redundant phrase. For example, the definition of the adjective *dynamic* is "a process or system...characterized by constant change, activity, or progress." Borrow *change* from the definition and turn it into *changing*, and you have *changing dynamic*, which is just an exquisitely redundant phrase. Or you can consult a thesaurus to find synonyms. For example, a synonym for *memorable* is *notable*. Turn *notable* into an adverb and you get the phrase *notably memorable*. Of course, if something is notable, it is also memorable.

A. ______________________ accelerate
B. ______________________ adventure
C. ______________________ appreciate
D. ______________________ environment
E. ______________________ fascinating
F. ______________________ illuminate
G. ______________________ inconceivable
H. ______________________ incredible
I. ______________________ memorable
J. ______________________ opportunities

3. Here are some sentences containing redundant phrases. Cut the extra word or words. Each sentence has at least one redundant phrase. Feel free to fix others if you see them.
   A. After extensive debate, the committee reached a definite decision regarding the allocation of funds for the public health initiative.
   B. During the course of the election campaign, the candidate's stance on key issues evolved in response to changing public opinion and political dynamics.
   C. In his proposal, the candidate spells out in detail his plan for economic reform, outlining specific policy measures and their expected outcomes.
   D. In political science, understanding the basic fundamentals of democratic governance is essential for analyzing the effectiveness of different political systems in promoting citizen participation and accountability.
   E. The close proximity of the two countries has led to frequent border disputes, highlighting the importance of diplomacy and conflict resolution in maintaining regional stability.
   F. The decision to postpone the vote on the bill until later reflects the government's recognition of the need for further consultation and deliberation with stakeholders.
   G. An analysis of the nation's past history reveals recurring patterns of political instability following economic crises.
   H. The formation of policy often requires a consensus of opinion among political leaders, reflecting the complex interplay of competing interests and ideologies within a society.
   I. The government's decision to revert back to its previous foreign policy stance surprised many observers, signaling a shift in diplomatic strategy.
   J. The negotiation process for the trade agreement was arduous, but the document is now completely finished and ready for ratification by the participating countries.

4. Read through something you wrote at another time or for another class. Do you see any wordy or redundant phrases? Either those listed in this chapter or ones not listed here but that you are now prepared to see? Fix them.

CHAPTER 2

Passive Aggressive: On the Active and Passive Voice

Here is one sentence:

> The cow jumped over the moon.

And here is another version of it:

> The moon was jumped over by the cow.

At first glance, the sentences say more or less the same thing: there is a cow, there is the moon, and there is jumping. But on closer inspection, the sentences differ structurally and narratively. By structurally, I mean how the sentences are made and what they are made of. By narratively, I mean the story the sentences tell about a cow, the moon, and jumping. In this chapter, you will discover how these sentences differ, and why you should favor one (the first) over the other (the second). More specifically, you can expect to learn four rules:

1. Sentences come in one of two forms: the active voice and the passive voice.
2. Unless you have a good reason *not* to do so, you should use the active voice.

3. Sentencescanbeintheactivevoicebutnotuseactiveverbs.Toavoid confusion, we will call these verbs not active verbs but action verbs.
4. Unless you have a good reason *not* to do so, you should use action verbs.

These axioms (and this chapter) lead into the next one on action verbs.

The Active and Passive Voice

Start with the distinction between the active and the passive voice. To understand the difference, you have to know a little grammar. Not a lot, just a little. Textbooks will tell you that many sentences follow a subject-verb-object (S-V-O) pattern. That is true enough. However, I find it easier to think in terms of action. A sentence usually has three parts: an actor, an act, and the acted upon. Most sentences proceed from the actor to the act to the acted upon. Like this:

> Actor---------->Act---------->Acted Upon

Here is a sentence that follows that pattern:

> The tornado leveled the town.

In this sentence, *the tornado* is the actor: the person, place, or thing that does something. The act is *leveled*, what the tornado does. Finally, there is the acted upon, the part of the sentence that receives the action of the actor. In this case, *the town* bears the brunt of what the actor does. It is what the tornado leveled. In more conventional terms, *the tornado* is the subject; *leveled* is the verb; and *the town* is the object.

The sentence above is in the active voice because its subject (the tornado) performs the action described by the verb. What did the tornado do? It leveled. What leveled? The tornado. In most sentences, the subject is the actor, and it comes first. Or it should. We can now fill out our diagram:

> Actor (Subject)---------->Act (Verb)---------->Acted Upon (Object)

By contrast, sentences in the passive voice *turn the acted upon into the subject of the sentence*. Rendered in the passive voice, the sentence about the tornado and the town would look like this:

> The town was leveled by the tornado.

The content of these sentences remains the same. A tornado leveled a town. But instead of making the actor the subject of the sentence, instead of placing the actor first, sentences in the passive voice give pride of place to the acted upon. In this sentence, that is the town.

You can think of sentences as stories. In the active-voice version of the sentence, the story is about the tornado and what it did. In the passive-voice version, the story is about the town and what happened to it. The acted upon (the town) is promoted to the subject, while the actor (the tornado) is shuffled off to the end of the sentence.

You can recognize the passive voice not just because it makes the acted upon the subject of the sentence. Passive-voice sentences also give themselves away because they take an additional verb and a different verb tense. A sentence in the passive voice requires a helping verb, usually one of the *to be* verbs: *is, are, was, were, been, being, become.* So, instead of saying "leveled," the sentence in the passive voice has to say "was leveled." A sentence in the passive voice also takes a past tense verb. That rule is hard to see in the passive-voice sentence about the tornado because its verb ("leveled") is already in the past tense. But consider these paired sentences:

> The dog guards the house.

The verb (*guards*) is in the present tense. By contrast, a passive-voice version of the sentence would read thus:

> The house is guarded by the dog.

Instead of *guards* (present), we now have a *to be* verb (*is*) linked to a past tense verb (*guarded*).

The other giveaway in a passive-voice sentence is a preposition. Because in the passive voice the acted upon comes first, the sentence needs to connect the actor back to the acted upon. Usually, the connection is the preposition *by*. The moon was jumped over *by the cow*. The town was leveled *by the tornado*. The house was guarded *by the dog*. You need to be careful, though. Some writers, especially those trying to obscure who did what, will write a passive-voice sentence that leaves out the *by* clause.[1]

Rarely are sentences so basic as *The tornado leveled the town* or *The house was guarded by the dog*. To recognize whether a sentence is in the active or passive voice, you sometimes have to do some excavating. Consider this sentence:

> Some books written for children, especially those supposed to violate social norms, are targeted by school boards, thereby restricting

> the accessibility of diverse narratives for young readers and distorting the literary landscape of young adult literature.

What is the verb in this sentence? Or, put differently, what is the action? Do not be fooled. A lot of words look like verbs ("written," "violated," "distorting"), but only one word fulfills the function of a verb. If you have trouble seeing it, try finding the actor. Who is doing what? Or, if that is still not clear, ask a more basic question. What is happening in this sentence? Some books written for children are being targeted (and, presumably, banned). So, the verb is *targeted*. Who is targeting books? School boards. Chisel away at it, and you have a sentence that looks like this:

> Some books written for children...are targeted by school boards....

Is this sentence in the active or passive voice? We have two ways of knowing. First, we can figure out the actor, the act, and the acted upon and see whether the actor is the subject of the sentence. In this sentence, who is the actor? School boards. What do school boards do? They target. And what do they target? Books written for children. Is the actor (*school boards*) the subject of the sentence? Does it come first? No. The acted upon (*some books written for children*) is the subject. The sentence is in the passive voice.

The second method for determining whether a sentence is in the active or passive voice involves examining its verb. Remember, sentences in the passive voice require specific verbs:

1. A *to be* helping verb: is, are, was, were, been, being, become.
2. Wed to a past tense verb.

What is the verb in the school-board sentence? *Are targeted.* Does the verb have a *to be* helper? Yes. *Are.* Does it have a past tense verb? Yes. *Targeted.* Finally, although this test is not foolproof, does the sentence have the preposition *by* after the verb? It sure does. *By the school board.* The sentence is guilty as charged.

Use the Active Voice

But why speak of guilt and innocence when it comes to active- and passive-voice sentences? Why go to so much trouble figuring out whether a sentence is in the active or passive voice. Who cares?

The answer is because readers usually find it easier to follow active-voice sentences than passive-voice ones. Most of the stories we tell move from cause to effect:

> I solved the puzzle using only my wits.

What is the cause? I solved. What is the effect? A solved puzzle. Cause (me solving) leads to effect (solved puzzle). By contrast, sentences in the passive voice move from effect (solved puzzle) to cause (me solving it):

> The puzzle was solved by me using only my wits.

Unlike the active-voice version of that sentence, the passive-voice one requires some cumbersome disassembly and reassembly. We learn of the effect (*a solved puzzle*) before we learn of the cause (*me solving it*).

Similarly, the sentence about books for children being targeted by school boards asks less of a reader when we turn it from a passive-voice sentence into an active-voice one:

> School boards target some books written for children, especially those supposed to violate social norms, thereby restricting the accessibility of diverse narratives for young readers and distorting the literary landscape of young adult literature.

This revision illustrates why readers find it easier to follow active-voice sentences. If you look back at the passive-voice version, it takes a long time to get from the subject of the sentence (*books written for children*) to the verb (*are targeted*). In other words, readers do not find out *what* is happening in the sentence until midway through it. By contrast, the active-voice sentence gets right down to business: *School boards target*. Everything that follows just fills out what school boards target and the consequences of their doing so.

In addition to mirroring how most human beings think, sentences in the active voice require fewer words and are therefore more concise. Conversely, sentences in the passive voice take more words (a *to be* helping verb and a prepositional phrase) and therefore seem looser. The active-voice sentence about the tornado uses five words: *The tornado leveled the town*. The passive-voice sentence about the town uses seven: *The town was leveled by the tornado*.

Sentences in the active voice are also, well, more active. More vivid. In the active-voice version of the tornado sentence, the tornado levels from the start. The passive-voice version of the sentence delays the action. It takes an additional word (*was*) to get to the critical verb (*leveled*) and often a prepositional phrase (*by the tornado*) to get to the actor. It therefore takes longer to paint the full picture of what happened, what the sentence is trying to depict.

Hence rule number two: Unless you have a good reason *not* to do so, you should use the active voice.

What are the good reasons not to use the active voice? Or, stated positively, when *should* you use the passive voice? In his magisterial *Garner's Modern English Usage*, Bryan A. Garner lists six occasions:

1. When the actor is unimportant.
2. When the actor is unknown.
3. When you want or need to hide the actor's identity.
4. When you need to put the punch word at the end of the sentence.
5. When the focus of the passage is on the thing being acted upon.
6. When the passive simply sounds better.[2]

All of these reasons are good ones, but I cannot keep all of them in my head while writing or, for that matter, revising. As a result, I tend to only follow rule number five: when the focus of the passage is on the thing being acted upon. Or, as E. B. White put it: "The need to make a particular word the subject of the sentence will often...determine which voice to use."[3]

Consider our original sentences about the tornado leveling the town. In the paragraph from which it might come, ask yourself, am I telling a story about the tornado? Or am I telling a story about the town? Here is a paragraph about the tornado:

> The tornado leveled the town. It went on to destroy the fireworks factory. Then it skipped the cow pasture—thank God—only to touch down again at the grain silo.

And here is a paragraph about the town:

> The town was leveled by the tornado. Its shopping mall was razed to the ground. Its historical district is ruined beyond repair. The town will need millions of dollars to rebuild.

If your story is about what something does, like a tornado leveling a town, then use the active voice. If your story is about what is done to something else, like a town leveled by a tornado, then feel free to use the passive voice. That flexibility is why the psychologist and linguist Stephen Pinker likens the writer to a cinematographer and sentence voice to a camera angle. By using the active or passive voice, the writer can "direct" what the reader sees first and, therefore, what the reader sees most.[4] If you want the reader to see the actor (*the tornado*), make it the subject of the sentence. If you want the reader to see the acted upon (*the town*), make it the subject of the sentence.[5]

In sum, if you use the passive voice, do so deliberately and not by default. Too often, however, writers use the passive voice for no reason at all. Save it for when it matters.

To Be or Not to Be

In graduate school, I had a professor who encouraged his students to underline every *to be* verb or one of its variants (*is, are, was, were, been, being, become*) in their essay and, if possible, substitute a more active verb. That is good advice, and I will offer something like it in the next chapter, but it may unfairly malign the reputation of *to be* verbs. So let me say it plainly. Just because every sentence in the passive voice requires a *to be* verb *does not mean* every sentence containing a *to be* verb is in the passive voice and, therefore, a problem waiting to be solved. Put differently, sentences in the active voice can use *to be* verbs. "Hope is the thing with feathers," Emily Dickinson writes. That sentence uses *is*. But it is in the active voice. It may be hard to see, but "hope" is the actor and, therefore, the subject in the sentence. What does hope do? It *is* the thing with feathers. Rewrite Emily Dickinson at your peril.

To be verbs can also signal continuing action, in which case they very much have a place in writing. Take this sentence:

> The president is deciding between several potential nominees for the vacant Supreme Court seat, a decision that will likely have significant implications for the country's legal landscape.

The sentence would not convey what it needs to convey if the writer substituted *decides* for *is deciding*. If the verb is *decides*, the sentence expresses a general procedure. Who decides? The president. If the verb is *is deciding*, then readers know the action is ongoing. It does not happen in general. It is happening now.

Closer to home, I have used *is* many, many, many times in this chapter. But I have only used the passive voice once.[6] All of which is to say that *to be* verbs have their place in writing. They especially come in handy when you need to define something or state that something is something else. Take this sentence:

> A dog is man's best friend.

I could replace the *to be* verb. Like so:

> A dog exists as man's best friend.

But what good would it do? None. It may even do harm.

That said, just as writers should prefer the active voice, so too should they prefer active verbs. For the sake of clarity, however, let us call these verbs not active verbs but action verbs. Action verbs emphasize what something does. Other verbs—we call them linking verbs—emphasize what something is. Compared to action verbs, linking verbs can seem lifeless. A linking verb does not convey an action. Instead, it links the subject to a description of that subject. Compare this sentence:

> The car is up on concrete blocks.

To this one:

> The car perches on concrete blocks.

Both sentences are in the active voice, but *perches* is a more interesting, more dynamic verb than *is*. The action verb *perches* offers an image. (The car as bird.) The linking verb *is* does not. Even if you wrote, "The car is perched on concrete blocks," you bury the action. Think of it this way. Your job as a writer is not done just because most or all of your sentences are in the active voice. Your job is done when most or all of your sentences are in the active voice *and* use lively action verbs. The next chapter explains why.

Exercises

1. Which of these sentences is in the active voice and which in the passive voice? Underline the words that lead you to conclude what you do.
   A. Archaeologists unearthed the ancient city's ruins during their latest excavation.

B. The book was written by Mark Twain.
C. The anthropologist analyzed artifacts excavated from the ancient burial site to understand burial practices and cultural beliefs.
D. The concept of the "self" has been debated by philosophers for centuries.
E. The poet Homer crafted the epic poems the *Iliad* and the *Odyssey* during the eighth century BCE.
F. The effects of the therapy were studied extensively over a period of several years.
G. The novel was translated into over fifty languages, highlighting its global appeal.
H. The researchers administered surveys to a random sample of households to assess their attitudes toward government policies.
I. The play was directed by a renowned theater director known for his innovative approach to staging.
J. Scholars have debated the interpretation of this religious text for centuries.

2. Turn these active-voice sentences into passive-voice ones.
   A. The Pilgrims founded Plymouth Colony in 1620.
   B. George Washington led the Continental Army during the American Revolutionary War.
   C. The Founding Fathers drafted the Articles of Confederation in 1777.
   D. Lewis and Clark explored the western territories of the United States from 1804 to 1806.
   E. Abraham Lincoln conducted the famous debates with Stephen A. Douglas during the Illinois Senate race of 1858.
   F. Theodore Roosevelt held the office of President of the United States from 1901 to 1909.
   G. Franklin D. Roosevelt implemented the New Deal programs during the Great Depression in the 1930s.
   H. The Montgomery bus boycott began in 1955 when Rosa Parks refused to give up her seat to a white man.
   I. Martin Luther King Jr. delivered his iconic "I Have a Dream" speech during the March on Washington for Jobs and Freedom in 1963.
   J. Neil Armstrong and Buzz Aldrin walked on the moon during the Apollo 11 mission in 1969.

3. Turn these passive-voice sentences into active-voice ones.
   A. The Declaration of Independence was written by Thomas Jefferson.
   B. The Emancipation Proclamation was issued by President Abraham Lincoln during the Civil War.
   C. The United States Constitution was signed by delegates at the Constitutional Convention in 1787.
   D. The Louisiana Purchase was negotiated by President Thomas Jefferson in 1803, doubling the size of the United States.
   E. The Gettysburg Address was delivered by President Abraham Lincoln during the American Civil War.
   F. The Civil Rights Act of 1964 was signed into law by President Lyndon B. Johnson, prohibiting discrimination based on race, color, religion, sex, or national origin.
   G. The Manhattan Project was led by American scientists during World War II, resulting in the development of the atomic bomb.
   H. The landmark Supreme Court case *Brown v. Board of Education* was decided in 1954, overturning segregation in public schools.
   I. The Marshall Plan was implemented by the United States to aid European countries in rebuilding after World War II.
   J. The women's suffrage movement in the nineteenth century was led by courageous activists fighting for equal voting rights.

4. Below are ten sentences about the Constitution and its framers. Use five of the sentences to write a paragraph that features the framers as the subject. Compose these sentences in the active voice. For this paragraph, you may have to turn some passive-voice sentences into active ones. Then use five of the sentences to write a paragraph that features the Constitution (or its characteristics) as the subject. Compose these sentences in the passive voice.
   A. The framers of the Constitution, including notable figures like James Madison, Alexander Hamilton, and Benjamin Franklin, were convened in Philadelphia during the Constitutional Convention of 1787.
   B. The Constitution of the United States, ratified in 1788, is regarded as the supreme law of the land, having been established to provide a framework for the nation's government.

C. Their primary goal was to address the weaknesses of the Articles of Confederation and to create a more effective system of governance.
D. A system of checks and balances was established by the framers to balance power between the federal government and the states.
E. The separation of powers among three branches of government—the legislative, executive, and judicial branches—was outlined in the Constitution.
F. Through compromise and debate, a document was crafted by the framers that established principles of democracy, including the protection of individual rights and freedoms.
G. The Bill of Rights, added to the Constitution in 1791, guarantees essential liberties such as freedom of speech, religion, and the right to a fair trial.
H. Provisions for amendments were included in the Constitution, indicating the framers' foresight in allowing for the document's adaptation to changing times and circumstances.
I. Despite differing viewpoints and backgrounds, remarkable unity and commitment to creating an enduring government were demonstrated by the framers.
J. The enduring legacy of the Constitution is found in its ability to serve as a foundation for democracy, providing a framework for governance that has guided the United States for over two centuries.

5. Read through something you wrote at another time or for another class. Do you see sentences in the passive voice? Is there a reason for them to be in the passive voice? If not, change them to the active voice.

CHAPTER 3

Lights, Camera, Action Verbs!

Although Bill Martin Jr. and Eric Carle published *Brown Bear, Brown Bear, What Do You See?* nearly sixty years ago, it remains one of the most popular board books for parents to read to their children. To the question what does he see, Brown Bear famously answers, "I see a red bird looking at me."[1] Although it may not look like it, that response illustrates virtually everything you need to know about how to write a sentence.

You already learned the following terms in the previous chapter on the active and passive voice, but a review never hurts. Sentences, including the one by Brown Bear, often have the following structure:

> Subject----->Verb----->Object

A subject is who or what the sentence is about, usually a noun, pronoun, or noun phrase. A verb expresses an action, occurrence, or state of being. When the verb is an action, the object is the recipient of that action. You can identify the object of a sentence by finding the verb and asking *What* or, in rare cases, *Whom*?[2] Here is the Brown Bear version of that structure:

> Subject [I]----->Verb [see]----->Object [*see what?* a red bird looking at me.]

If you remember the book, the red bird sees a yellow duck, the yellow duck sees a blue horse, the blue horse sees a green frog, and so on, all following the same basic structure.

As writers start to compose more sophisticated sentences, many of those sentences continue to take a subject-verb-object form. For example, here is a sentence from a ChatGPT essay on *Hamlet* and the theme of betrayal:

> Shakespeare explores the complexities of betrayal and its consequences, highlighting the destructive nature of deceit and disloyalty.

This sentence looks a lot more complicated than the Brown Bear one, but it follows the same pattern:

> Subject [Shakespeare]----->Verb [explores]----->Object [*explores what?* the complexities...]

Hamlet, Hamlet, what do you see? I see a murderous uncle looking at me.

Trouble arises when writers substitute complex subjects for simple ones; trade action verbs like *explores* for *to be* verbs like *is*; and pile up heaps upon heaps of prepositional phrases. That is how you end up with a sentence like this one:

> The existential quandary of what truly "is" in the intricate tapestry of Shakespeare's *Hamlet* is inexorably intertwined with the thematic exploration of betrayal, as characters grapple with the complexities of loyalty and deceit in a world where the line between truth and falsehood is blurred.

That sentence makes a lot of noise, but it does not cast a lot of light. It fits into a subject-verb-object pattern, but it makes that structure almost unrecognizable:

> Subject [the existential quandary of what truly "is" in the intricate ...]----->
> Verb [is]----->
> Object [*is what?* inexorably intertwined with the thematic exploration of betrayal...]

Instead of a simple subject like *Shakespeare*, the writer has chosen a convoluted noun phrase for a subject. That longwinded noun means it takes readers much longer to get to the verb of the sentence. Until readers do, they have to keep in mind the subject of the sentence, what it is about, which is harder to do when it is not *Shakespeare* or *Hamlet* but *the existential quandary* of whatever. When readers do reach the verb, they do not find a sturdy one like *explores* but a rickety one like *is*. And the object, well, the less said about it the better.

In this chapter, you will learn how to write clear, concise, and lively sentences. You can train yourself to write sentences like these from the start.

But that does not happen overnight. In the meantime, if you focus too much on how you write, you may never get around to writing what you need to write. That is why the principles set out in this chapter work coming and going. They can guide you as you compose sentences, and they can help you revise the sentences you have already composed. The guidelines are deceptively modest:

1. Keep your subjects consistent and simple.
2. Get to verbs as quickly as possible.
3. Make those verbs as lively as possible.
4. Guard against too many prepositions.

I would love to devote a section to each of these principles and proceed logically from the first through the fourth. But like organisms in an ecosystem, in this case the ecosystem of a sentence, you can only understand one principle in relation to others. As a result, these discussions inevitably interact with each other.

Keep Your Subjects Simple and Your Verbs Close

The subject of a sentence is what the sentence is about. In all but a few cases, subjects are nouns (or noun phrases), which can be a person, place, thing, idea, or quality. Or subjects can be pronouns standing in for a person, place, thing, idea, or quality. Regardless, readers find it easier to keep track of simple subjects. In the following sentences, the subjects become increasingly complex. As they do, the sentences become increasingly unreadable:

1. Impressionism is characterized by its emphasis on capturing the effects of light and color.
2. Impressionism as an art movement is characterized by its emphasis on capturing the effects of light and color.
3. Impressionism as an art movement of the late nineteenth century is characterized by its emphasis on capturing the effects of light and color.
4. Impressionism as an art movement of the late nineteenth century in France is characterized by its emphasis on capturing the effects of light and color.
5. Impressionism as an art movement of the late nineteenth century in France, which was led by revolutionary painters like

Renoir, Monet, and Pissarro, is characterized by its emphasis on capturing the effects of light and color.

6. Impressionism as an art movement of the late nineteenth century in France, which was led by revolutionary painters like Renoir, Monet, and Pissarro, who were indifferent to the criticism aimed at them from the traditional art world, is characterized by its emphasis on capturing the effects of light and color.
7. Impressionism as an art movement of the late nineteenth century in France, which was led by revolutionary painters like Renoir, Monet, and Pissarro, who were indifferent to the criticism aimed at them from the traditional art world, and whose paintings would eventually sell for tens of millions of dollars, is characterized by its emphasis on capturing the effects of light and color.
8. Impressionism as an art movement of the late nineteenth century in France, which was led by revolutionary painters like Renoir, Monet, and Pissarro, who were indifferent to the criticism aimed at them from the traditional art world, and whose paintings would eventually sell for tens of millions of dollars and hang in the most prestigious museums, is characterized by its emphasis on capturing the effects of light and color.

And so on. These sentences suffer from two related problems. First, the writer tries to pack too much information into the subject of the sentence. Prepositions (*as, of, in, by, to, from, for, of, in*) combine with other clauses (*which was led, who were indifferent, and whose paintings*) to weigh down the subject (*Impressionism*) and nearly sink it beneath the load.

The second problem is born from the first. Note how as the subject takes on more and more words, the verb shifts farther and farther away from the subject. In the first sentence, the subject lives next door to the verb. By sentence eight, a staggering fifty-five words separate subject from verb. Few readers can walk that long of a tightrope from subject to verb. Most will plunge to their deaths, figuratively speaking, and curse the writer as they fall.

You can fix both problems—elaborate subjects and delayed verbs—in one stroke. Split up the long sentence into shorter ones:

> Impressionism as an art movement of the late nineteenth century in France is characterized by its emphasis on capturing the effects of light and color. **It** was led by revolutionary painters like Renoir, Monet, and Pissarro, who were indifferent to the criticism aimed at them from the traditional art world. **Despite the critics**, their

> paintings would eventually sell for tens of millions of dollars and hang in the most prestigious museums.

Each of these sentences now has a discrete subject. Or, better said, each of these discrete subjects now has its own sentence. Notice too that the subjects in these sentences appear closer to the verbs that indicate what they do. In the first sentence, eleven words separate the subject (*Impressionism*) from its verb (*is*). In the second sentence, the verb (*was led*) immediately follows its subject (*It*). So too the final sentence: *Their paintings* [noun] *would eventually sell* [verb]. The last sentence can place its subject next to the verb by placing a prepositional clause (*Despite the critics*) at the start of the sentence. The writer could have pulled off the same trick with the first sentence: "As an art movement of the late nineteenth century in France, Impressionism is characterized...." As is, though, the sentence still reads well.

These examples illustrate three out of the four rules for writing clear, concise, and lively sentences:

1. **Keep your subjects consistent and simple.**
2. **Get to verbs as quickly as possible.**
3. Make those verbs as lively as possible.
4. **Guard against too many prepositions.**

Here is what can happen when writers ignore these rules. The subject of the following sentence sprawls across the page:

> The potentially detrimental effects of chronic stress resulting from prolonged exposure to adverse life events, such as poverty, abuse, or discrimination, are often a factor in the development of psychological disorders in vulnerable populations.

Prepositions (*of, from, to*) and clauses (*such as*) complicate the subject and push the verb farther and farther away, so much so that when readers do finally get to the verb (*are*), they have likely forgotten what the subject is. When you find prepositions overwhelming your subject, simplify the subject and rewrite the sentence. Sometimes it will take two simple sentences to replace one complicated one. For example:

> The potentially detrimental effects of chronic stress **result** from prolonged exposure to adverse life events, such as poverty, abuse, or discrimination. **These detrimental effects** are often a factor in the development of psychological disorders in vulnerable populations.

Notice what has happened in the first sentence. I have taken the word *resulting* and transformed it into a verb. You will see more of these transformations below.

You could do still more to fix these sentences. The first sentence, in particular, still seems wordy and weighed down by prepositions (*of, from, to*). You could probably cut *The potentially detrimental effects of* and skip straight to *chronic stress* without losing much at all. (Does chronic stress lead to other effects besides detrimental ones?) That would make the subject even simpler. The revised paragraph might look like this:

> ~~The potentially detrimental effects of chronic~~ **Chronic** stress **can** result from prolonged exposure to adverse life events, such as poverty, abuse, or discrimination. ~~These detrimental effects are~~ **It is** often a factor in the development of psychological disorders in vulnerable populations.

Notice that I have changed the subject of the second sentence from *These detrimental effects* to the pronoun *It*, which now stands in for the subject of the first sentence, *chronic stress*. As the chapter on the active and passive voice showed, readers struggle when they have to keep track of more than two or three subjects in any one paragraph. Part of keeping your subjects simple, then, is keeping them consistent.

Before moving on to discuss how verbs can make or break your sentence, consider one last warning about prepositions. Thus far, they have caused trouble when they needlessly complicate the subject of a sentence and therefore delay your verb. However, prepositional phrases can also get up to no good when they come *after* verbs. That is because readers are dazed by sentences that feature more than two or three prepositions, especially when those prepositions follow a weak verb like *is*. You can experience this struggle for yourself in the following sentence. Good luck.

> Capitalism is an economic system in which the means of production are owned and controlled by individuals and businesses and in which goods and services are exchanged in markets based on supply and demand.

That sentence makes me motion sick. The problem is not a complex subject. It could not be simpler than *Capitalism*. Nor is the problem that it takes too long for the subject of the sentence to find its verb. The two appear next to each other: *Capitalism is*. The problem is all the prepositions (*in, of, by, in, in, on*) and conjunctions (*and, and, and, and*) that come after the verb.

Prepositions lead readers through a maze of phrases and, as in a maze, readers can easily get lost. They often have to retrace their steps, which means doubling back and starting from the beginning. Usually more than once. Try this one:

> Illegal immigration is a result of individuals seeking refuge from poverty or violence in their home countries and involves the crossing of borders without authorization or inspection.

Here too the verb follows closely on the heels of a simple subject: *Illegal immigration is*. Yet all the prepositions (*of, from, in, of, without*) cause the sentence to twist and turn like a roller coaster. Add in all the conjunctions (*or, and, or*) and readers do not stand a chance of making sense of this sentence on a first pass.

As with the earlier sentences, you can fix these sentences easily enough. Just break them into multiple sentences:

> Capitalism is an economic system in which the means of production are owned and controlled by individuals and businesses**.** ~~and in which~~ **In it**, goods and services are exchanged in markets based on supply and demand.

Or:

> Illegal immigration is a result of individuals seeking refuge from poverty or violence in their home countries. ~~and~~ **It** involves the crossing of borders without authorization or inspection.

Those sentences will not set the world on fire, but at least they provide enough light to read by.

So, when it comes to guarding against prepositional phrases, you should do so regardless of where those phrases fall in a sentence. If your sentence has more than three prepositions that occur before the verb, or more than three that appear after, consider rewriting the sentence. Specifically, consider breaking the sentence into two or more shorter sentences. In chapter seven on sentence variety, I advise writers to occasionally insert a short sentence into their prose. Far from feeling contempt for them, readers often appreciate a short sentence—or even just a shorter sentence. It gives them a chance to catch their breath.

Make Those Verbs as Lively as Possible

Go back to the first of our sentences that foreshadowed the perils of proliferating prepositional phrases:

> Impressionism is characterized by its emphasis on capturing the effects of light and color.

What is the verb in this sentence? *Is*. Although it may seem bold, in reality *is* connects more than it does assert. That is why grammarians refer to it and other verbs like it as linking verbs. These verbs do not contain an action but link the subject to a group of words that renames the subject. Hence, as I suggest in the previous chapter on the active and passive voice, you can occasionally use *is* or other linking verbs to define or describe something. *A vote for the bill* is *a vote for justice. An electron cloud* is *a probabilistic region around an atomic nucleus where electrons are likely to be found.* But rely on *is* too much and your sentences start to wilt. Fortunately, you can often perk up these wilting sentences rather easily. In the sentence about Impressionism, could you substitute a single verb for the verb phrase *is characterized by its emphasis on* that would mean more or less the same thing? And by more or less the same thing, I mean the same damn thing. I will give you a hint. The verb is hiding in plain sight, except it wears the costume of a noun. Here:

> Impressionism ~~is characterized by its emphasis on~~ **emphasizes** capturing the effects of light and color.

This substitution accomplishes a couple of things at once. It preserves the proximity of subject to verb. It trades a dead verb (*is*) for a livelier one (*emphasizes*). In doing so, it makes the sentence more concise. It goes from fifteen words to nine. Crucially, two of the words it eliminates are prepositions: *by* and *on*. All in all, the sentence becomes clearer, shorter, and more dynamic. What is there not to like?

This substitution illustrates the last two of the four principles, especially the third:

1. Keep your subjects consistent and simple.
2. Get to verbs as quickly as possible.
3. **Make those verbs as lively as possible.**
4. Guard against too many prepositions.

In the previous chapter, I distinguished between sentences in the active voice and sentences that use active verbs. To avoid confusion, I proposed calling these verbs not active verbs but action verbs. I added that unless you have a reason not to do so, you should use action verbs. Now you can see why.

Think about how you would revise this sentence, which comes from a philosophy paper generated by ChatGPT:

> *The Republic* is an examination of the concept of justice within the context of an ideal society.

The subject is fine. It could not get much simpler than the title of a book. And the verb (*is*) is close enough to the subject. Indeed, it could not get any closer. Nevertheless, the sentence trails off—and with it goes readerly attention. Why? Because it has four prepositional phrases after the verb: *of the concept, of justice, within the context, of an ideal society.* How could you fix the sentence? You could try playing around with the prepositional phrases or turning the sentence into two sentences. Before you do that, though, try swapping an action verb for a dead one:

> *The Republic* ~~is an examination of~~ **examines** the concept of justice within the context of an ideal society.

If you get rid of the *is*—or never write it in the first place—you can trim the prepositions down to size and make the sentence readable again.

The Lazarus Strategy

How do you fix a sentence that depends on a verb like *is*? As we did by substituting *examines* for *is an examination of*, often you can simply turn a noun back into a verb. To find the hidden verb, look for forms of the verb *to be*: *is, are, was, were, been, being, become.* Then rescue the verb from the clutches of the nearby noun. For example, here is a sentence from a paper on climate change:

> The results of this study about climate change and habitat loss are in agreement with previous findings in the field.

And here it is with a lost-and-found verb:

> The results of this study about climate change and habitat loss ~~are in agreement~~ **agree** with previous findings in the field.

Here is a sentence from a paper on *Native Son*:

> In Richard Wright's *Native Son*, the character of Bigger Thomas becomes an embodiment of the dehumanizing effects of racism and poverty in 1930s America.

And here it is with a borrowed but lively verb:

> In Richard Wright's *Native Son*, the character of Bigger Thomas ~~becomes an embodiment of~~ **embodies** the dehumanizing effects of racism and poverty in 1930s America.

The lesson is straightforward enough. Find the *to be* verb, cut it, then turn the accompanying noun into an action verb.

I think of this approach to fixing sentences as the Lazarus Strategy. In the Gospel of John, Jesus raises Lazarus from the dead after four days in the tomb. Unlike Jesus, you cannot resurrect the dead, but you can resurrect a verb that has been buried in the grave of a *to be* verb and a noun. All you have to do is turn the entombed verb into its lively equivalent:

1. The theory of social conflict, developed by Karl Marx, ~~is an explanation of~~ **explains** how inequalities in power and resources, rooted in the capitalist mode of production, can lead to societal tensions and struggles between social classes.

2. Dante's *Divine Comedy* ~~is a blend of~~ **blends** profound theological insights, vivid poetic imagery, and intricate philosophical concepts, making it a masterpiece of world literature.

3. The surge in consumer electronics spending during the Black Friday weekend ~~is a reflection of~~ **reflects** both heightened economic optimism, driven by recent job market improvements, and the strategic marketing campaigns that have incentivized early holiday shopping behaviors among consumers.

4. Toni Morrison's novel *Beloved* ~~is a haunting and poignant portrayal of~~ **hauntingly and poignantly portrays** the psychological and emotional scars of slavery on individuals and communities.

5. The inclusion of mindfulness meditation in Christian prayer practices ~~is an adaptation of~~ **adapts** Eastern spiritual traditions to Western religious contexts.

The Lazarus strategy works with other *to be* verbs than just *is*. You just have to match the tense of the new verb to the tense of the *to be* verb.

6. The concept of dualism ~~was an explanation of~~ **explained** the mind-body problem by positing that even though the mind and body are distinct substances with different natures, they nevertheless interact to form human experience.

7. The burial customs observed by the ancient civilization ~~are a document of~~ **document** their beliefs about the afterlife and the spiritual realm.

8. The paintings of the Dutch Golden Age ~~were an illumination of~~ **illuminated** the societal values and cultural themes of the time.

9. The studies have ~~been a showcase of~~ **showcased** the complex interplay between genetics and environmental factors in shaping personality traits.

10. The model of "separate spheres," which emerged in the nineteenth century, ~~became a justification for~~ **justified** excluding women from the public sphere of politics and business.

Even the very wordiest of subjects in these sentences can stand if they have a lively verb to prop them up. For example, the subject of the following sentence consists of three prepositional phrases, which would ordinarily set off alarm bells. But the sentence still works if you revitalize the dead verb:

> The underrepresentation of women in leadership positions in the tech industry ~~is a demonstration of~~ **demonstrates** persistent gender biases and systemic barriers that hinder women's advancement in STEM fields.

Writers can get away with a lot if they have an action verb like *demonstrates* instead of a linking verb like *is*.

You can follow this principle—make your verbs as lively as possible—in two ways. You can use it to fix the sentences you have already composed. After you have written *is a demonstration of*, for example, you can return to the sentence and substitute *demonstrates*. Eventually, however, you can teach yourself to stop writing *is a demonstration of* in the first place and start writing *demonstrates* from the start. In that case, you will no longer have to resurrect verbs. You just keep them from dying.

Afterword: Bringing Subjects Back from the Dead

This chapter recommends that you keep your subjects consistent and simple, but that advice meets its match if no readily identifiable subject appears in the sentence. Often, this situation arises when writers lean on words like *it* and *there*. For example:

1. There is a deep-seated belief in many cultures that life is a sacred gift.
2. There are several key factors that contribute to the stability of a democratic system.
3. It is widely accepted among historians that the Renaissance was a period of profound cultural transformation in Europe.
4. It is evident that the concept of the 'other' is a recurring theme in postcolonial literature, challenging traditional notions of identity and power.

In addition to wordiness, these sentences suffer from the vagueness that attends words like *there* and *it*. In the sentences above, I could guess what they refer to, but I would only be guessing. Fortunately, no one has to guess because the sentences can do just as well without them.

Indeed, you can see how little work these words do by appreciating how easily you can simply eliminate them. For that to happen, though, you need to resurrect the subject as much as you do the verb:

1. ~~There is a deep-seated belief in many~~ **Many** cultures **believe** that life is a sacred gift.

2. ~~There are several~~ **Several** key factors ~~that~~ contribute to the stability of a democratic system.

3. ~~It is widely accepted among historians~~ **Historians accept** that the Renaissance was a period of profound cultural transformation in Europe.

4. ~~It is evident that the~~ **The** concept of the "other" ~~is a recurring theme in~~ **recurs throughout** postcolonial literature, challenging traditional notions of identity and power.

Notice that each of these sentences follows the same introductory pattern: *There are...that* and *It is...that.* You can almost always save such sentences by striking the introductory chatter.

> ~~It is widely recognized that technological~~ **Technological** advancements have reshaped the dynamics of interpersonal communication.

The literary scholar Richard A. Lanham calls these "Blah Blah is that" sentences. No one is listening (or needs to listen) to the Blah Blah.[3]

One more thing. Look at sentence number three above. Even after resurrecting its subject and verb, the sentence still contains a *to be* verb: *was.* Such is the power of simple subjects and action verbs that they can support a *to be* verb in the object. Often more than one. For example:

> ~~There is a common misconception~~ **Many people mistakenly believe** that poverty is solely a result of individual failures and is therefore a problem only individuals can solve.

You could turn that sentence into two sentences, and maybe you should, but even as one it remains coherent.

Once you know how to revise subjects and verbs, you can turn to sentences where you have to do more than just tinker with the subject and verb to make them run. For example, how would you fix this sentence:

> Effective communication is crucial in addressing and dismantling the structures of racism that persist in society.

The phrase *is crucial in* does not contain a verb that, Lazarus-like, can be resurrected from the grave. You need to add something if you want to delete the *is* verb. Ask yourself, what is the action at the heart of this sentence? *Communication.* And who is—or should be—undertaking this action? Once you answer these questions, you need to invent (or borrow) a subject and a verb for the occasion:

> ~~Effective communication is crucial in addressing and dismantling~~ **We must communicate effectively if we hope to address and dismantle** the structures of racism that persist in society.

These sentences suggest that the first rule for writing sentences (Keep your subjects consistent and simple) might benefit from a qualification: **You may need to create a new subject before you can fix the sentence**. It might also benefit from a qualification to the qualification: **More often than not, you will want to make people (or groups of people) the subjects of sentences**. As a rule, sentences work better when a person—and not a thing or idea—is the subject.

It took me a long time to learn how to write sentences according to the principles I outline in this chapter. (I see I am still learning because I just used a sentence that began with *it*.) Let me try again: I worked long and hard to learn how to write sentences according to the principles I outline in this chapter. Until I did, I applied these principles to the sentences I had already written. But the process feeds back on itself. Revise enough sentences and you start to write sentences you do not need to revise. It is a neat trick. Almost as neat as a talking bear.

Exercises

1. Take one of the sentences below and complicate the subject by adding more and more prepositional phrases and conjunctions. Write five sentences. For inspiration, see the series of sentences about Impressionism on pages 36–37.
   A. Taylor Swift is one of the most successful and influential musicians of her generation.
   B. LeBron James is a cultural icon whose impact extends beyond the basketball court.

   Once you have complicated the subject of the sentence as much as you possibly can, fix the final sentence by breaking it into shorter sentences. Make sure that your subject and verb are divided by no more than five words.

2. Take the starting sentences from Exercise one and add prepositional phrases and conjunctions *after* the verb. Write five new sentences. Fix the final sentence by breaking it into shorter sentences. For inspiration, see the sentences on capitalism and illegal immigration on pages 39–40.

3. Fix the following five sentences by resurrecting a verb from a noun.
   A. The movie *To Kill a Mockingbird* is an adaptation of Harper Lee's novel of the same name, translating its themes and characters to the screen.

B. In many religions, the microcosm of the individual is a mirror of the macrocosm of the universe.
C. The concept of supply and demand is a description of the relationship between the availability of a good or service (supply) and the desire of consumers to purchase it (demand).
D. One of the key sentences of the Second Amendment is its reference to a "well regulated Militia."
E. The development of a child's personality is dependent upon genetic predispositions and environmental influences.

4. These five sentences need a new subject as well as a new verb before you can fix them.
   A. There is a long-standing debate in philosophy about the nature of reality and whether it is ultimately material or immaterial.
   B. It is evident that social inequality is a pervasive issue in contemporary society, impacting access to resources and opportunities based on factors such as race, class, and gender.
   C. There are differing perspectives within anthropology on the impact of globalization on traditional cultural practices.
   D. It is widely argued that gender is a complex and multifaceted social construct, shaped by a variety of factors including culture, biology, and individual identity.
   E. Studying these artists is a way to gain a deeper understanding of their creative process, influences, and the historical context in which they worked.

5. Take something you have written at another time or for another class and find the three worst sentences. The sentences should have a sprawling subject; use *is* or another form of *to be* as their verb; and have entirely too many prepositions. Use the principles outlined in this chapter to fix them.

CHAPTER 4

Lost Connections: Modifiers, Parallelism, Transitions, and Vague Pronouns

In his great one-man show, *Springsteen on Broadway*, Bruce Springsteen tells a wonderful story about how he and his bandmates, hoping to get discovered by a record producer, drove from New Jersey to San Francisco in seventy-two hours. The group left in two cars, but somewhere around Nashville, the cars got separated. In the days before cell phones, if you lost someone, as Springsteen puts it, "they're fucking lost." Gone. You could only hope to find them again once everyone arrived wherever they were going.

Like the two cars Springsteen and his friends drive, this chapter is about lost connections, when sentences or parts of sentences lose track of each other and leave readers wondering how one thing relates to another. Specifically, the chapter takes up the issues of misplaced and dangling modifiers, parallelism, transitions, and vague pronouns. If the chapter has a motto, it would borrow one from the novel *Howards End* by E. M. Forster: "Only connect."

Modifiers

What is wrong with this sentence:

> Lasting 381 days, Rosa Parks refused to give up her bus seat to a white man, sparking the Montgomery Bus Boycott.

As it reads now, the clause *Lasting 381 days* modifies Rosa Parks. (By modify, I mean the grammatical definition of the term, which is to provide more information about another item in a sentence, in this case a noun.) But Rosa Parks did not last 381 days. She lived—she lasted—until 2005. Rather, *Lasting 381 days* should modify the Montgomery Bus Boycott. You can fix the sentence by rephrasing the clause and moving it elsewhere:

> ~~Lasting 381 days,~~ Rosa Parks refused to give up her bus seat to a white man, sparking the Montgomery Bus Boycott, **which lasted 381 days**.

In the first sentence, the clause *Lasting 381 days* is called a misplaced modifier. Like your keys or your phone when you cannot find them, a misplaced modifier has been left where it should not have been. In the language of this chapter, it has lost its connection to the noun or noun phrase it should modify.

The following example is silly, but it makes the point:

> I saw the lost dog driving down the street.

The *speaker* was driving down the street. Not the lost dog. To fix a misplaced modifier, you re-place it in the sentence:

> **Driving down the street,** I saw the lost dog ~~driving down the street~~.

As a rule, you should place modifiers as close as possible to the noun or noun phrase they modify. Take this sentence:

> Having been composed over two centuries ago, some historians question the relevance of the Constitution to modern life.

Some historians are indeed old, but they were not composed over two centuries ago. You would revise the sentence like so:

> Some historians question the relevance of the Constitution, **which was composed over two centuries ago, to modern life**.

To speak formulaically, if clause X modifies the noun or noun phrase Y, place X as near as you can to Y.

Many style books use the terms misplaced modifiers and dangling modifiers interchangeably, but there is a difference between the two that writers would do well to remember. A misplaced modifier, as I say, is a sentence that can be fixed by moving the modifier closer to the noun it should modify. In sentences like these, you have all the elements you need—noun or noun phrase, modifier—you just have to arrange them in the right order. By contrast, a dangling modifier is a modifier that not only does not modify what it should, but what it should modify does not appear in the sentence at all. Here is an example:

> Written and directed by Orson Welles, audiences were initially confused.

Obviously, *audiences* were not written and directed by Orson Welles. Rather, one of his films was. Yet the title of that film goes unnamed. In these types of sentences, not only has one thing lost connection to another. Instead, one side of the connection has been lost entirely, like a remote control without a television. In order to fix the sentence, the writer must supply the noun the modifier modifies:

> Written and directed by Orson Welles, ***Citizen Kane*** initially confused audiences.

Better.

Here is another example. Think about what goes wrong and how to fix it:

> From studying the Rosetta Stone, the history of ancient Egypt is illuminated.

The history of ancient Egypt cannot study the Rosetta Stone. Something else, something unnamed, did. You can fix the sentence by adding a noun the dangling modifier can grab onto:

> From studying the Rosetta Stone, **linguists** can illuminate the history of ancient Egypt.

When modifiers are misplaced or dangling, readers can usually figure out what you mean. Lost dogs do not drive cars. People do. But you should not force readers to make connections you should have made for them.

Parallelism

Here is one of the sentences from the introduction to this chapter:

> Specifically, the chapter takes up the issues of misplaced and dangling modifiers, parallelism, transitions, and vague pronouns.

All of the "issues" in this list follow the same grammatical form. They are nouns with the occasional adjective. By contrast, this revision mixes their forms:

> Specifically, the chapter takes up the issues of **repairing** misplaced and dangling modifiers, parallelism, **how to write transitions**, and vague pronouns.

You can see this mixture more easily in an actual list:

1. Repairing misplaced and dangling modifiers
2. Parallelism
3. How to write transitions
4. Vague pronouns

All of these items are nouns or noun phrases. But the first ("Repairing misplaced and dangling modifiers") and the third ("How to write transitions") take a different shape than the second and the fourth. To fix the sentence, you need to make all of the items in the list parallel. By parallel, I do not mean the geometrical definition of the word. ("Parallel lines never meet.") Rather, I mean existing at the same time in a similar way ("A parallel universe.")

To make items in a list parallel, you have to put them in the same form. If you wanted to follow the pattern of "Repairing misplaced and dangling modifiers," your list would look like this:

1. Repairing misplaced and dangling modifiers
2. Making items in a list parallel
3. Writing transitions
4. Avoiding vague pronouns

Each item begins with a gerund (an -ing word). Or you could follow the "How to" pattern of the "How to write transitions." Thus:

1. How to repair misplaced and dangling modifiers
2. How to make items in a list parallel
3. How to write transitions
4. How to avoid vague pronouns

Some items in a list work better in one form than another. For the sake of concision, my original sentence just lists more or less bare nouns. In any case, like should go with like. In doing so, you link—in the language of this chapter, you connect—items in a list.

A sentence with only two items may illustrate the point more clearly:

> In many societies, it is often easier to conform to traditional gender roles than challenging them.

The first item in the list is "to conform" and the second is "challenging." These take different shapes. In order to fix them, you need to make them the same shape:

> In many societies, it is often easier to conform to traditional gender roles than **to challenge** ~~challenging~~ them.

What might you do with a sentence like this one:

> A Shakespearean sonnet, also known as an English sonnet, includes the following characteristics: it has fourteen lines; the poet writes in iambic pentameter; an abab cdcd efef gg rhyme scheme; a use of poetic devices such as metaphors, similes, and personification to enhance the meaning and emotion of the poem.

The universe of items in this list are not parallel but chaotic. They follow four separate forms. Notice too how the last item stands out because it is longer than the others. Not only do items in a list need to be parallel; they need to be roughly the same length. How can order be restored? Give each item the same form:

> A Shakespearean sonnet, also known as an English sonnet, includes the following characteristics: **it has** fourteen lines; **it is written in** iambic pentameter; **it follows** an abab cdcd efef gg rhyme scheme; and **it uses** poetic devices such as metaphors, similes, and personification.

Each entry in the list follows an *it-something* form (It has...it is written in... it follows...it uses.) The last item has also been trimmed to match the length of the other items in the list. If you need to say more about poetic devices, say them in the next sentence or elsewhere.

If you wanted to make the list more concise, you could delete the *it-somethings* and just list the items:

> A Shakespearean sonnet, also known as an English sonnet, includes the following characteristics: fourteen lines; iambic pentameter; an abab cdcd efef gg rhyme scheme; and poetic devices such as metaphors, similes, and personification.

Regardless of how you do it, you want to make sure all the items in a list—like cadets mustered for inspection—wear the same uniform.

What difference does it make whether items in a list are parallel or not? It matters for the sake of coherence. Readers can more easily keep track of items in a list when they share the same form. But it also matters musically, strange as that may sound. Just as lines of a sonnet follow a pattern of stressed and unstressed syllables, a list of items should also follow an audible pattern. When it does not, the list sounds discordant. When it does, readers not only see the connection between words; they can hear it too.[1]

Transitions

Watch this: If parallelism connects the dots among items in a list, then transitions connect the dots between paragraphs in an essay.

The previous sentence is a transition. It links what has come before in a piece of writing (the topic of parallelism) to what will come next (the topic of transitions). Specifically, my transition follows an if-then pattern. A transition does not have to follow that pattern, but it does have to connect before and after. Without transitions, a piece of writing will sound like a clash of scattered thoughts. With them, it can blend into a coherent whole. You can think of a transition as a bridge that connects one side of a river to another. In this analogy, a reader is like a hiker. You, the writer, have to offer safe passage from one idea to another. If you do not, a reader has to leap from idea to idea. Readers do not like to leap.

Transitions come in two forms: those that connect sentences and those that connect paragraphs. (Or, in the case of the transition that leads off this discussion, those that connect sections.) You have a better chance of understanding transitions between sentences if you understand transitions between paragraphs. Pay attention to the boldfaced sentence of the second paragraph:

> Libertarianism is a political philosophy that emphasizes individual liberty, autonomy, and minimal government intervention in both personal and economic matters. At its core, libertarianism holds that individuals should be free to live their lives as they choose, as long as they do not infringe on the equal rights of others. This philosophy advocates for a limited role of government, with the belief that excessive government intervention can lead to infringements on individual freedom.
>
> **One of those freedoms is economic.** Libertarianism emphasizes free markets and limited government regulation of economic activities.

The sentence that begins the second paragraph connects the discussion of the previous paragraph to what will be the discussion of the next paragraph. It does so by picking up a key word ("freedom") from the final sentence of the previous paragraph and using it to build a bridge to the next paragraph. Readers can now walk across that bridge from one paragraph to the next.

You can appreciate the power of transitions by taking one away. Here are the above paragraphs without the transition:

> Libertarianism is a political philosophy that emphasizes individual liberty, autonomy, and minimal government intervention in both personal and economic matters. At its core, libertarianism holds that individuals should be free to live their lives as they choose, as long as they do not infringe on the equal rights of others. This philosophy advocates for a limited role of government, with the belief that excessive government intervention can lead to infringements on individual freedom.
>
> Libertarianism emphasizes free markets and limited government regulation of economic activities.

These paragraphs make sense. But they have lost their connection to each other. The second paragraph is supposed to offer an example of individual freedoms. It should go from the general to the specific. Without a transition, without the bridge from one paragraph to another, readers have to supply the connection. They may not be able to, and they may resent having to do so.

You do not always have to invoke a keyword to join one paragraph to the next. Sometimes a simple word or phrase will suffice:

> Libertarianism is a political philosophy that emphasizes individual liberty, autonomy, and minimal government intervention in both personal and economic matters. At its core, libertarianism holds that individuals should be free to live their lives as they choose, as long as they do not infringe on the equal rights of others. This philosophy advocates for a limited role of government, with the belief that excessive government intervention can lead to infringements on individual freedom.
>
> **For example**, libertarianism emphasizes free markets and limited government regulation of economic activities.

Writers have all sorts of words like *for example* at their disposal. I do not mean synonyms for *for example* but, rather, conjoining words that can reveal the logic between one paragraph and the next. You need only pick the right one.

According to ChatGPT, which is adept at calculating language use, here is a curated list of ten of the more commonly used transitions and their purposes:

1. **However**: to contrast or to contradict.
2. **Therefore**: to conclude or to sum up.
3. **Moreover**: to add information.
4. **Nevertheless**: to contrast or to insist despite conceding.
5. **Meanwhile**: to indicate time or to contrast.
6. **As a result**: to conclude or to state an outcome.
7. **Finally**: to conclude a series or argument.
8. **For example**: to illustrate.
9. **In other words**: to rephrase or to clarify.
10. **Similarly**: to compare.

To these, I would add a couple more:

1. **In brief**: to repeat in fewer words.
2. **Indeed**: to make the abstract concrete.
3. **In sum**: to summarize or to conclude.
4. **By contrast**: to, well, contrast.

Here let me offer a word of warning. Sensing that they need to use a transition, writers will sometimes choose one that is not up to the task. In other words, beware that all-purpose word *Another*. The transition *Another* is in reality no transition at all. It just tosses another log on the fire. It sometimes takes the form of *Another idea*:

> Libertarianism is a political philosophy that emphasizes individual liberty, autonomy, and minimal government intervention in both personal and economic matters. At its core, libertarianism holds that individuals should be free to live their lives as they choose, as long as they do not infringe on the equal rights of others. This philosophy advocates for a limited role of government, with the belief that excessive government intervention can lead to infringements on individual freedom.
>
> **Another idea** is that libertarianism emphasizes free markets and limited government regulation of economic activities.

A transition like *Another idea* could go anywhere in an essay. You might think that such versatility would recommend it, but instead it nullifies it. Transitions should be specific to the paragraphs they connect. Otherwise, they do not function as transitions at all.

You can often use the same strategies to link sentences as you do to link paragraphs. (Note the transition.) Here is a paragraph from earlier in the chapter. I have boldfaced the transition words.

> Many style books use the terms misplaced modifiers and dangling modifiers interchangeably, but there is a difference between the two that writers would do well to remember. A misplaced modifier, **as I say**, is a sentence that can be fixed by moving the modifier closer to the noun it should modify. **In sentences like these**, you have all the elements you need—noun or noun phrase, modifier—you just have to arrange them in the right order. **By contrast**, a dangling modifier is a modifier that not only does not modify what it should, but what it should modify does not appear in the sentence at all.

This paragraph mixes key words ("sentences like these") with simple phrases ("as I say"; "By contrast"). Here is the paragraph without the transitions:

> Many style books use the terms misplaced modifiers and dangling modifiers interchangeably, but there is a difference between the two that writers would do well to remember. A misplaced modifier is a sentence that can be fixed by moving the modifier

> closer to the noun it should modify. You have all the elements you need—noun or noun phrase, modifier—you just have to arrange them in the right order. A dangling modifier is a modifier that not only does not modify what it should, but what it should modify does not appear in the sentence.

Without transitions, the paragraph sounds comparatively lifeless. Instead of being led on a guided tour, the reader is dropped off in the middle of a city without a map. Transitions between paragraphs and sections matter more than transitions between sentences. But careful writers try to offer both.

This, That, and the Other Thing

I have saved the most important discussion—the most frustrating example of lost connections in writing—for last. I speak of that suffocating nightmare, the vague pronoun.

A pronoun, you will remember from elementary school, is a word that stands in for a noun (or a noun phrase). The noun it stands in for is called its antecedent. Like so:

> Napoleon initiated widespread educational reforms. He laid the groundwork for the modern French educational system, emphasizing merit and equal opportunity for all students.

In the second sentence, the pronoun is *He* and the antecedent is *Napoleon.* If you began the second sentence with *Napoleon* instead of *He,* the two sentences would sound repetitious:

> Napoleon initiated widespread educational reforms. Napoleon laid the groundwork for the modern French educational system, emphasizing merit and equal opportunity for all students.

Keep going, and the sentences would begin to sound like a skipping record:

> Napoleon initiated widespread educational reforms. Napoleon laid the groundwork for the modern French educational system, emphasizing merit and equal opportunity for all students. Napoleon established a foundation for future advancements in

> science, literature, and the arts. In doing so, Napoleon contributed to a flourishing cultural environment in France.

Enough about Napoleon.

Usually, readers have no problem understanding which noun a pronoun represents. In this case, *He* can only stand in for *Napoleon.* There is no other person—no other he—whom the pronoun could refer to.

The same goes for even slightly more capacious pronouns like *this.* That is, if the previous sentence is simple enough, a pronoun like *this* can usually make it clear what it refers back to.

> Emily Dickinson challenged the conventions of nineteenth-century poetry. This would later put her at odds with critics who valorized those conventions.

The *This* that opens the second sentence is a little more ambiguous than the *He* that began the second Napoleon sentence. Unlike *he* or *she* or *they,* which stand in for a person or a group of people, the pronoun *This* can stand in for all sorts of other nouns, whether a place, a thing, an idea, or a quality. On the one hand, that flexibility is useful. On the other hand, it can confuse. In the Emily Dickinson sentence above, most readers will understand that the *This* refers to her challenge to the conventions of nineteenth-century poetry.

When nouns and noun phrases start to proliferate, however, they can start to overwhelm an indeterminate pronoun like *this.* To borrow from the theme of this chapter, a pronoun can start to lose its connection to its antecedent. Take this sentence:

> Hannah Arendt's exploration of the human condition, as seen in works like *Eichmann in Jerusalem,* revealed her deep concern with the political implications of human behavior and her awareness of the fragility of democratic societies. This underscored her belief in the importance of civic responsibility and the dangers of apathy in the face of political oppression.

Consider the *This* at the beginning of the second sentence. Does it refer to:

1. Arendt's exploration of the human condition
2. Her deep concern with the political implications of human behavior

3. Her awareness of the fragility of democratic societies
4. All of the above

I have no idea. Nor will a reader. The writer may know perfectly well what *This* refers to. Because they do know, however, it never occurs to them to specify which noun or noun phrase the pronoun takes the place of. They simply expect *This* to be as obvious to readers as it is to them. But readers cannot read minds. They can only read the words on the page. And when the words on the page lose their connection to other words on the page, readers will inevitably think to themselves, *This what?* What is this person talking about? Which of these things does *This* refer to?

To fix this *This* problem, you need to reunite the pronoun to its antecedent. You can do so by specifying which antecedent the pronoun is referring to:

> Hannah Arendt's exploration of the human condition, as seen in works like *Eichmann in Jerusalem*, revealed her deep concern with the political implications of human behavior and her awareness of the fragility of democratic societies. This **awareness** underscored her belief in the importance of civic responsibility and the dangers of apathy in the face of political oppression.

By adding the word *awareness*, the writer signals to the reader which part of the previous sentence the *This* invokes. It invokes *her awareness of the fragility of democratic societies.* If the writer wants the *This* to refer to more than one noun, they can substitute *These* for *This* and add a specific antecedent:

> Hannah Arendt's exploration of the human condition, as seen in works like Eichmann in Jerusalem, revealed her deep concern with the political implications of human behavior and her awareness of the fragility of democratic societies. ~~This~~ **These fears** underscored her belief in the importance of civic responsibility and the dangers of apathy in the face of political oppression.

In this case, you name a synonym for the antecedents you want the pronoun to stand in for. In the second sentence, I want the antecedent of *This* to refer to *her deep concern with the political implications of human behavior* and *her awareness of the fragility of democratic societies.* A synonym for *concern* and *awareness* is *fear.* Hence *These fears.*

Above I wrote that so long as the noun or noun phrase that precedes *This* is simple enough, a writer can get away with *This* and *This* alone. That said, few readers will complain if a writer draws a line connecting *This* and the noun phrase it stands in for.

> Emily Dickinson challenged the conventions of nineteenth-century poetry. This **defiance** would later put her at odds with critics who valorized those conventions.

Here too you find a synonym for the antecedent, which in this case is *challenged the conventions of.* What is a synonym for *challenged*? *Defiance.* Or perhaps *creativity.* Maybe *boldness.* Regardless, when in doubt, err on the side of the specific.

In chapter six, I confess that few errors irritate me as much as this one: "Early Christians faced persecution for their beliefs, however, their faith and community grew steadily." You need at least a semi-colon—and not just a comma—before *however*; otherwise, the sentence is a run-on. One of the errors that might irritate me more—and I am not alone—is when a vague pronoun like *this* begins a sentence without clearly indicating what it refers to. In short, this *this* business has to stop.

In fact, writers would do well to reconnect all the lost words—misplaced and dangling modifiers, items in a list, sentences and paragraphs without transitions, and vague pronouns—that, like two cars, can get separated from each other somewhere around Nashville.

Exercises

1. Write two sentences on any of the following topics:
   A. A canceled flight
   B. A pothole
   C. A piano concert
   D. A lawsuit
   In the first sentence, include a misplaced modifier. In the second, a dangling modifier. For example, here are two sentences about a birthday party:
   For dessert, she served cupcakes to the children on paper plates.
   For dessert, she served the children.
   The first example is a misplaced modifier. She does not serve cupcakes to the children on paper plates—in which case the children not on paper plates were out of luck—but cupcakes on paper plates to children. The second example is a dangling modifier.

It lacks what the modifier *For dessert* modifies. Presumably, she does not serve up children. That would be gruesome. Rather, she serves *cupcakes* on paper plates to children. Once you have written your sentence, fix it. Or swap sentences with someone else.

2. Fix these misplaced and dangling modifiers.
   A. Trying to paper over their differences, the Fugitive Slave Act was passed in 1850.
   B. Surviving centuries, the museum carefully preserves ancient artifacts.
   C. Having struggled with mental illness, the Virginia Woolf novel *Mrs. Dalloway* provides a unique perspective on the human psyche.
   D. Written into law in 1850, many Northerners found the Fugitive Slave Act objectionable.
   E. Maneuvering for political advantage, the district boundaries were redrawn to influence election outcomes.

3. Begin a sentence "This morning, I..." and then list four things you did this morning. Make them not parallel. Then make them parallel.

4. Fix these examples of non-parallel sentences.
   A. Judaism is characterized by its monotheistic belief in one God, the Torah, and observing traditional Jewish laws and customs.
   B. Rhyme is a poetic device that enhances musicality, creating rhythm, and the memorability of verse.
   C. In the realm of penal systems, it is often more challenging to rehabilitate offenders than incarcerating them.
   D. Gospel music played a pivotal role in the civil rights movement by providing spiritual strength, it spread messages of hope and resilience, and its mobilization of communities for social change.
   E. Critics of fracking argue that it can lead to groundwater contamination, the air being polluted, and minor earthquakes that can nevertheless be measured on the Richter scale.

5. See the paragraphs below on loneliness. Write two separate transitions for the start of the second paragraph that connect it to the previous paragraph. For the first transition, use a key word from the final sentence of the previous paragraph. For the second, use

a simple word or phrase to do so. (You can consult the list on page 56.)

Loneliness can have profound and detrimental effects on mental health. Research has shown that prolonged loneliness is associated with an increased risk of depression, anxiety, and other mental health disorders. It can also lead to feelings of low self-esteem and worthlessness, further exacerbating these conditions. The impact of loneliness on mental health is not limited to emotional well-being; it can also affect cognitive function, leading to difficulties in concentration and memory.

Studies have found that lonely individuals are more likely to experience cardiovascular issues, such as high blood pressure and heart disease. Loneliness can also weaken the immune system, making individuals more susceptible to infections and illnesses. Additionally, the stress caused by loneliness can contribute to inflammation in the body, which is linked to a variety of chronic conditions.

6. In the blank spaces below, create transitions that link a sentence to the previous one. Some transitions call for using a simple word or phrase (see page 56). Others call for using a key word from the previous sentence. In the case of the opening sentence of the second paragraph, create a transition that links that paragraph to the previous one.

Participant observation is a qualitative research method where researchers immerse themselves in a particular social setting to observe and participate in the activities of the group being studied. _____________ allows researchers to gain a deep understanding of the culture, behaviors, and interactions of the group in their natural environment. _________________________________ _______________, researchers can observe firsthand how people behave, how they interact with each other, and how they make sense of their world. ___________ is particularly useful in fields such as anthropology and sociology, where the goal is to understand the social and cultural dynamics of a group or community.

____ __________________, researchers can build rapport and trust with the group members, leading to more authentic and insightful data. ______________ in the social setting helps researchers uncover nuances that may not be apparent through other research methods, such as interviews or surveys. ___________, a researcher studying a religious community might attend services, participate in rituals, and engage in everyday conversations to gain a comprehensive understanding of the community's beliefs and practices. ____ _________ is a key strength of participant observation, allowing researchers to capture the complexity and depth of social phenomena.

7. Fix these vague pronouns (and the accompanying verb) by filling in the blanks.
   A. Propaganda is a form of communication that is used to influence the attitudes, beliefs, and behaviors of a group of people. This _________________________ is often used in politics, advertising, and public relations to shape public opinion and promote a particular agenda.
   B. Religion plays a crucial role in many communities, providing a sense of identity, belonging, and moral guidance to its members. This ____________________ often serves as a foundation for community values and traditions, shaping social interactions and collective rituals.
   C. Economic inequality refers to the unequal distribution of income and wealth among individuals or groups within a society. This _________ often leads to social and economic challenges, such as limited access to education, healthcare, and opportunities for upward mobility.
   D. The use of social media platforms by influencers and celebrities can shape perceptions and influence trends among their followers. These __________________ often leads to depression.
   E. The colonization of indigenous lands by European powers had profound and lasting effects on native populations and their way of life. This __________________ imposed new laws and practices on what had been stable cultures.

CHAPTER 5

Better Late Than Never: On Clichés

Benjamin Dreyer, for years the lead copy editor at Random House, jokes that "Clichés should be avoided like the plague."[1] As a rule, it is good advice. Indeed, nearly every style manual, including this one, will warn you against using clichés. After I join the chorus for why you should avoid clichés, however, I would like to suggest that good writing can include a cliché or two. But only one or two.

Clichés come in one of three forms. The introductory gambit of "According to *Webster's Dictionary*" typifies the first kind. Writers may want to begin an essay with a definition, to make sure everyone understands what we will talk about before we start talking about it. But writers have used the phrase "According to *Webster's Dictionary*" (or its cousin, "*Webster's Dictionary* defines...") so often that the phrase now seems hopelessly derivative. Worse, its dullness can rub off on the writer who uses it, undermining their trustworthiness. A cliché like "According to *Webster's Dictionary*" invites your reader to ignore everything else you go on to write. If this writer does not know that "According to *Webster's Dictionary*" is stale, your reader may think, then why should I care what else they have to say? Might it be similarly stale? Indeed, all clichés, not just ones like "According to *Webster's Dictionary*," run the risk of staleness. They repeat what has repeatedly been thought and said. By definition, they make you sound like everyone else. Yet as I argue in the introduction to this book, one aim of writing should be to sound like yourself.

You can think of phrases like "According to *Webster's Dictionary*" as plain clichés. Unlike the other kinds of cliché, these never had any figurative or metaphorical value. Like a favorite concert T-shirt, they just got worn out.

Here are some other examples of plain clichés, especially those that you might be tempted to include in an essay:

> In modern society...
> Throughout history...
> In conclusion...

Most of these phrases are not just clichés but also silly. For example, *throughout history* is redundant. If something has occurred *throughout history*, you do not need to flag it as happening throughout history. It has, by definition, always happened. Instead of writing something like *Throughout history, human beings have dreamt of an afterlife*, you can just write *Human beings have always dreamt of an afterlife. In conclusion* is just plain irritating. Do you know why I, the reader of your essay, do not need to be told that a paper has reached its conclusion? Because there are no more pages.

The second type of cliché could just as easily be called jargon. Jargon refers to words or expressions that are used by a particular profession or group. One of my hobbies is wristwatches. If you visit online watch forums, you will discover all sorts of words you may have never heard before: balance wheel, bezel, beats per second, crown, complication, escapement, lug, lug-to-lug, mainspring, movement, power reserve, rotor, seconds per day, tourbillon, and so on. I am also an English professor and therefore part of a field that over the years has developed its own share of jargon. (I would prefer not to get into it.) Some style guides discourage using any jargon, but you can get away with jargon when your reader is familiar with it. In the right hands, it can function as a sort of concision. On watch forums, instead of saying the number of times a balance wheel oscillates back and forth in one second, I can just say beats per second. Or bps.

Some jargon, however, can slip into the realm of cliché, in which case it can, like clichés in general, displace original thought. That is especially true with business and administrative jargon. Unless you work in an office, you may not recognize these overused phrases. But if you do, or if you plan to, you should prepare yourself for them: action item, bandwidth, best practice, circle back, deep dive (or, more recently, drill down), deliverable, going forward, leverage, pivot, touch base. Do not be surprised if you encounter a paragraph like the following one:

> Given our current bandwidth, it is crucial that we follow best practices to manage our time efficiently. In our next team meeting, we will discuss action items related to improving our customer service

> process. We need to drill down into the details to ensure every deliverable is met on schedule. Going forward, we should leverage our existing resources to maximize productivity. If we encounter any obstacles, we may need to pivot our strategy accordingly. Before the meeting concludes, I would like to touch base with each department to confirm their progress and address any concerns. We will circle back to any unresolved issues the following week.

You can adopt one of two attitudes toward a paragraph like this one. You can, as I do, think it is as pretentious as it is wordy. What is the difference between "customer service process" and "customer service"? Why do we have to "follow best practices to manage our time efficiently" instead of just "managing our time efficiently"? What else could you "drill down into" except details? Generalities? Or you can accept, like you would accept jargon as it appears in a watch forum or in any other realm, that this is just the way that people in business and administration talk. I suspect, however, that if you were to rewrite the paragraph above without the jargon, you might impress people with your concision and clarity. Moreover, you might actually have to think about an issue instead of just burying it beneath an avalanche of clichés.

The third kind of cliché is the most common. These are phrases that may have once seemed vivid but, through overuse, have lost their verve. Consider a cliché like *fit the bill.* It means to be suitable for a particular purpose. Its context is the theater, specifically vaudeville. A bill was a list of performers in a show. (Even today, if you see a show on Broadway, you receive a *Playbill* upon entry.) To *fit* (sometimes *fill*) *the bill* meant to fill out the list of performers. You already had a magician and a ventriloquist, but a plate spinner would really fit the bill. At some point in the past, some anonymous soul invented a phrase (*fit the bill*) that seemed so ingenious to those who heard it or read it that others started using it in other contexts. But eventually people repeated the phrase so often that it no longer summoned an image (playbills) but, rather, turned into just another empty saying. If every time a reader encountered the phrase *fit the bill* they imagined a poster or vaudeville playbill, if, that is, they could see its original metaphor, the phrase could live again. But since most readers do not think of a poster or a playbill, the phrase lies dead, buried in the mass grave of clichés.

Once a cliché no longer summons an image, it becomes much easier for writers to unknowingly join one cliché to another. We call these concoctions mixed metaphors. Take this sentence from a comparative literature paper:

> The protagonist's journey is a double-edged sword that paves the way for a final reckoning.

The problem here is that one dead metaphor ("double-edged sword") is followed by a different one ("paves the way"). If a writer stopped to think about the words they use, they would see that the sentence is at best illogical and at worst comic. A double-edged sword refers to a sword that cuts both ways—that is, it can have helpful and harmful effects for those who wield it. "Paves the way" is a different image. It refers to laying down a smooth road to make the going easier. One paves the way through a dense forest. But a journey cannot be a double-edged sword *and* something that paves the way. Worse, the clashing images can make it sound like the double-edged sword paves the way. That is quite an image. If you really wanted to play editor, you could say the sentence introduces a third metaphor. A "reckoning" summons images of counting. So, the sentence features a double-edged sword that paves the way toward a final reckoning. Oh my.

Even if you keep your metaphors straight and not mixed, they also need to stay fresh. Here are some other previously lively phrases that are now dead-on-arrival:

> Ignorance is bliss.
> Opposites attract.
> Read between the lines.
> The more the merrier.
> The calm before the storm.
> Time heals all wounds.

Beginning writers may struggle to recognize a cliché as a cliché. A phrase like *time heals all wounds* may sound old to me but new to you. So, how do you know if something is a cliché or not? You have to trust your ear. Or you can ask someone whose writing you respect to read your work. They may find clichés that you cannot see. In any case, if you find yourself writing a phrase that sounds familiar to you or someone else, you need to fix it.

But fix it how? Before I describe the options, note one strategy that does not fix a cliché: placing quotation marks around it or adding a phrase like *the proverbial.* Here is an example:

> When evaluating the effectiveness of educational practices, it is crucial to acknowledge that "actions speak louder than words."

I understand the impulse. A writer wants to signal that they know the phrase is a cliché but they intend to use it anyway. But putting a cliché in quotation marks does not make it any less of a cliché. It is still a cliché.

So, if you cannot quotation mark or *proverbial* your way out of a cliché, how can you fix it? You have four options:

1. You can delete the cliché.
2. You can translate the cliché into plain language.
3. You can invent a lively image or phrase to take the place of the dead one.
4. You can sacrifice one cliché to use another.

Many sentences work just fine without the cliché. Take this sentence: *At the end of the day, the United States must take bold action to address climate change.* You lose nothing by cutting "At the end of the day": *The United States must take bold action to address climate change.*

Each of the other three strategies requires a little more finesse. Consider a cliché like *the more the merrier*. It means fun is not a zero-sum game. As the number of people in a group increases, so does the fun. Two people can go to a dance and have fun; three people can go to a dance and have even more fun; and four people, well, now the fun can start. But if you translate *the more the merrier* into plain language (option two), you might substitute something even duller than the original cliché. Instead of *the more the merrier*, would you really want to write a phrase like *fun is not a zero-sum game*? Doing so might alienate readers more than the cliché.

The next option is to invent a lively image or phrase to take the place of the dead one. Instead of *the more the merrier*, how about *more people means more fun*? At least that preserves the alliteration that once made *the more the merrier* so pleasing. But if you write *more people means more fun*, your reader might wonder why you did not just write *the more the merrier*. That is what makes inventing new phrases for old ones so difficult. We already have a phrase for *more people means more fun*. It is *the more the merrier*. The phrase has moved into our language and defends its territory like a pack of wolves.

Your final option is to use the occasional cliché—with an emphasis on occasional. Here is a paragraph about crowdfunding generated by ChatGPT:

> The concept of crowdfunding has become increasingly popular in recent years, particularly for startups and small businesses. Crowdfunding involves raising money from a large group of people, often through online platforms, in order to fund a specific project or venture. By pooling resources, these entrepreneurs are able to access the capital they need to get their business off the ground, while also creating a community of supporters who are invested in their success.

Say you wanted to add a feisty last sentence to the end of this otherwise sedate paragraph. You could write (1) *In other words, crowdfunding is not a zero-sum game.* You could write (2) *In other words, more investors means more investments.* Or you could write (3) *When it comes to crowdfunding, the more the merrier.* The first sentence offers an accurate if rather dry summary of crowdfunding. The second is a decent substitute, though a bit redundant. I would argue that the third, the sentence that uses the cliché, outclasses the first two. And in doing so I would have powerful allies. No less a figure than H. W. Fowler, the crankiest of perhaps all style docents, wrote the following in the entry on clichés for his *A Dictionary of Modern English Usage*:

> [W]riters would be needlessly handicapped if they were never allowed to say that...someone had *his tongue in his cheek* or a *bee in his bonnet.* What is new is not necessarily better than what is old; the original felicity that has made a phrase a cliché may not be beyond recapture.[2]

In order to use a cliché, you have to signal to your reader that you know it is a cliché *and* that you know that *they* know it is a cliché. That means instead of using quotation marks around them, you should use them sparingly. Very sparingly. If you wanted to make *the more the merrier* the last sentence in the crowdfunding paragraph, you would first need to strike the phrase "off the ground" from the sentence that reads "the capital they need to get their business off the ground." "Off the ground" is a cliché. A phrase like "entrepreneurs are able to access the capital they need to *start* their business" works fine, and it clears the dance floor for a livelier cliché like *the more the merrier.*

Still not convinced? Consider this paragraph (on clichés no less!) from one of the leading writing handbooks for students:

> Steer clear of clichés, expressions so familiar that they have become trite (white as snow, the grass is always greener). Editors and writing instructors...prefer fresh and unique combinations of words rather than familiar and possibly overused phrases.[3]

Reader, what is the opening phrase of this paragraph, "steer clear," if not a cliché? The expression refers to a boat that should avoid some hazard—an outcropping of rocks, a shoal—lest it crash into it and sink. Yet how many people see boats and rocks when they encounter a phrase like "steer clear"? It is a dead metaphor. So, what happened to the "editors and writing instructors" who supposedly "prefer fresh and unique combinations of words rather than familiar and overused ones"? Were they asleep at the wheel of this ship? Maybe. But to me the error, if it is one, demonstrates two things: (1) We do not always agree on what counts as a cliché. To the writers and editors of this guidebook, "steer clear" is not trite and there is no reason to prefer an original phrase over it. (2) Since "steer clear" is the only cliché in the paragraph, perhaps it belongs after all. Maybe readers will recall the metaphor behind it: ships are like writers, clichés are like hazards, and both ships and writers would do well to avoid them. A writer more concerned about clichés could substitute "avoid" for "steer clear": "Avoid clichés, expressions so familiar...." But this editor and writing instructor is not convinced that the substitution would improve the sentence. If we can see a ship steering clear of rocks, the cliché gives us something to look at, which you cannot say for the lifeless "Avoid."

~~In conclusion,~~ The rule of *the more the merrier* does not apply to clichés. You can get away with one cliché, maybe two, but like puns you need to save clichés for when they will do the most good.

Exercises

1. These sentences suffer from mixed metaphors: two or more images that, like strangers in a movie theater, sit uncomfortably close to one another. Underline the images and clichés that form the mixed metaphors.
   A. The foundation of his argument begins to unravel as it drowns in a sea of contradictory evidence.
   B. The market was a powder keg waiting to explode, but policymakers managed to weather the storm by injecting liquidity into the system.
   C. The movement for gender equality gained traction, breaking the glass ceiling while planting seeds of change across society.
   D. The speaker's message was a lightning rod that sparked a wave of dialogue, but it quickly ran out of steam as the audience lost interest.
   E. In the work of the playwright Tom Stoppard, the dialogue dances like a flame, illuminating the complexities of human nature while anchoring the narrative in a whirlwind of philosophical inquiry.

2. Underline the clichés in these sentences. (There may be more than one.) Try to fix the sentences by using each of the first three strategies for rooting out clichés: cut it, translate it, or invent something better. Which strategy worked best?
   A. The economic recession is hitting the country hard, but there is light at the end of the tunnel as recovery efforts gain momentum.
   B. The phrase "divide and conquer" describes a key strategy employed by colonial powers to exert control over indigenous populations.
   C. The state faced many challenges in implementing the new policy, but every cloud has a silver lining, and there is hope that the policy will be better off because of these initial difficulties.

3. There are several clichés in the following paragraphs. Not everyone will agree on the same ones. Underline the clichés you see and then apply whichever of the four strategies (cut, translate, invent, or sacrifice one for another) you think will fix the sentence and paragraph best.

   Take the example of a business owner who is just starting out. They may have a vision for their company and a plan to make it successful, but they will face roadblocks along the way. Perhaps their initial marketing efforts fail to pay off, or they struggle to find the right man for the right job who will help grow their business.

   In these situations, it can be easy to become discouraged and retreat with your tail tucked between your legs. However, those who are able to stay the course are much more likely to achieve success. By learning from their mistakes and remembering that Rome wasn't built in a day, they can eventually build a thriving business that fulfills their wildest dreams.

4. Write a paragraph (four to six sentences) about artificial intelligence, political polarization, student debt, or any other subject you like. Include as many clichés as you can. Using the four strategies (cut, translate, invent, or sacrifice one for another), go back and fix what you have written.

5. Read through something you wrote at another time or for another class. Do you see any clichés? Underline them and then apply whichever of the four strategies (cut, translate, invent, or sacrifice one for another) you think will fix the sentence best.

CHAPTER 6

The Art of Joinery: Fragments, Run-On Sentences, and the Oxford Comma

As an English professor with stupidly too many books, over the years I have built my share of bookshelves. These are crude affairs, horizontal planks of wood screwed into vertical pieces and held together by a spine running up the back. My only nod to actual woodworking, what carpenters refer to as joinery, are so-called dado joints: grooves on the vertical planks of wood carved out with a router into which the horizontal planks sit.

No one would call my shelves beautiful. But they work. They hold books.

As with my bookshelves, this chapter concerns how to make and join things. Specifically, it shows you (1) how to create complete sentences and avoid fragmented ones; (2) how to join clauses within a sentence and avoid run-on sentences; and (3) how to join a list of items within a sentence. Like my bookshelves, sentences do not need to look beautiful. But they do need to do their job, which, in this case, is to hold your thoughts as neatly and solidly as a bookshelf holds books.

Sentence Fragments

Grammarians have defined a sentence in too many ways to count, but the simplest and most useful definition is the following: "a group of words containing a subject and a [verb] and expressing a complete thought."[1] For example, here is a sentence from an essay on the *Federalist Papers*:

> Alexander Hamilton advocated for a strong central government.

A subject is the person, place, or thing that does something. In this sentence, the subject is *Alexander Hamilton.* A verb is the action in a sentence, or what the subject does. In this case, the verb is *advocated.* And a complete thought is more easily defined by what it is not: it is not an incomplete thought. The following sentence has a subject and a verb. They are the same as those in the previous sentence. But the sentence does not express a complete thought:

> Although Alexander Hamilton advocated for a strong central government.

Although means *in spite of the fact that,* but this sentence does not follow through on that thought. Instead, it leaves readers hanging from a syntactic cliff. "Although what?" they will ask. What happened in spite of the fact that Alexander Hamilton advocated for a strong central government? The technical term for a construction—notice I do not say sentence—like this one is a subordinate or dependent clause. Such clauses often begin with words like *although, because, if, since, unless, whereas, while,* and so on. (These are called subordinating conjunctions.) Without a so-called independent clause for the dependent clause to depend on, the sentence does not express a complete thought. You may hear these fragments in particular referred to as fragmented clauses.

You have already seen a sentence that has a subject and a verb but does not offer a complete thought. (*Although Alexander Hamilton advocated for a strong central government.*) Here is another one:

> Because medieval art focused on religious themes.

Because means *for the reason that* or *since.* So, what happened because medieval art focused on religious themes? The sentence fragment withholds that crucial information. The revised sentence supplies it:

> Because medieval art focused on religious themes, **it often depicted Biblical narratives and saints in a symbolic and stylized manner**.

Notice that what comes after the dependent clause could stand on its own as a sentence:

> It often depicted Biblical narratives and saints in a symbolic and stylized manner.

In other words, it is an independent clause. You will want to keep this definition in mind for when the chapter turns to run-on sentences, below.

In addition to fragmented clauses, there are fragmented phrases. If a sentence consists of (1) a subject, (2) a verb, and (3) a complete thought, a fragmented phrase is a sentence that lacks one or more of these essential items. What is missing in this sentence that makes it a fragment of a sentence and not a whole one?

> Correlates with long-term cognitive health.

The sentence—or, better said, the fragment—lacks a subject. *What* correlates with long-term cognitive health? The writer does not say. Provide a subject and you have a complete sentence:

> **Exercise** correlates with long-term cognitive health.

Some fragments have subjects but lack verbs. For example:

> The impact of social media on identity formation.

This would-be sentence withholds what its subject (*The impact of social media on identity formation*) does. The revised sentence fills in the blank:

> The impact of social media on identity formation **has become a significant area of study in contemporary sociology.**

Sometimes sentences have words that look like verbs or, in other contexts, could function as verbs but are not in fact verbs. Here is one:

> The juxtaposition of the pastoral and courtly settings in *As You Like It* underscoring the theme of appearance versus reality.

Underscoring could form part of a verb phrase:

> The juxtaposition of the pastoral and courtly settings in *As You Like It* **is** underscoring the theme of appearance versus reality.

Of course, you could substitute *underscores* for *is underscoring* (see the chapter on action verbs) but *is underscoring* at the very least supplies a verb and creates a complete thought. By itself, however, *underscoring* does not act as a verb.

Some derelict sentences lack a subject *and* a verb *and* do not express a complete thought:

> Reflecting on the nature of existence.[2]

Who is reflecting on the nature of existence? Come to think of it, is "Reflecting" even a verb? (It is not.) And what does the unidentified subject do as a result of reflecting on the nature of existence? Hell if I know. To fix this fragment, you can add a subject and turn "Reflecting" into a proper verb:

> **Heidegger reflects** on the nature of existence.

Or you can treat "Reflecting on the nature of existence" as a phrase that modifies—that is, it offers additional information about—another element in the sentence. You can then attach the phrase to an independent clause:

> Reflecting on the nature of existence, **Heidegger argued that being-in-the-world is fundamental to human experience.**

In this sentence, *Reflecting on the nature of existence* modifies Heidegger. It functions as a sort of dependent clause in as much as it depends on the independent clause that follows.

As these examples illustrate, you have a couple of options when it comes to fixing a sentence fragment. But first you must diagnose the problem.

1. **If a sentence lacks a subject, give it one:**
   ~~Shaped~~ **Rituals shaped** communal identity with early Christian communities.

2. **If a sentence lacks a verb, invent one:**
   China ~~with~~ **has** a rich cultural history spanning thousands of years.
   Or adapt one:
   The ritualistic practices observed during the initiation ceremony ~~highlighting~~ **highlight** the significance of rites of passage in shaping individual and communal identities within tribal culture.

3. **If a sentence lacks a complete thought because it begins with a subordinating conjunction (*although*, *because*, *if*, *since*, *unless*, *whereas*, *while*), alter the subordinate or dependent clause.**

Take this sentence:

Although Picasso revolutionized modern artistic expression.

You can fix it in one of two ways:

A. Delete the subordinating conjunction and add a subject:
~~Although revolutionizing~~ Picasso revolutionized modern artistic expression.

B. Keep the dependent clause and lean it against an independent clause:
Although Picasso revolutionized modern artistic expression, **his early works were not widely appreciated in his time**.

4. If a sentence lacks a subject, a verb, and a complete thought...

A. Add a subject and adapt a verb:
~~Revolutionary in~~ **The Beatles revolutionized** both sound and style.

B. Let the fragment modify the subject:
Revolutionary in both sound and style, **the Beatles** transformed the landscape of popular music.

If all of this—subordinating conjunctions, dependent and independent clauses, modifiers—feels overwhelming, just remember that a complete sentence needs a subject, a verb, and a complete thought. Provide these and the fragments disappear.

No one likes a fragment. If I owe you ten dollars and pay you nine, you will rightly object. If I promise you a whole cookie and give you half, you will moan about the injustice of it all. So, too, readers. They want the sentences they have coming to them. They do not want fragments of them.

Run-On Sentences

You might think that if sentence fragments do not have enough of something (subject, verb, complete thought), then run-on sentences would have too much of something. But that is not quite right. Rather, like a sentence fragment, a run-on sentence lacks something. It does not lack a subject, verb, or complete thought. Instead, it lacks the right kind of punctuation. Specifically, a run-on sentence consists of two independent clauses that, unlike the planks in my bookshelves, have not been sufficiently joined.

As you learned in the previous section, an independent clause is just another term for a complete sentence. That is, it has a subject, a verb, and it expresses a complete thought:

> Early Christians faced persecution for their beliefs.

The subject is *Early Christians*, the verb is *faced*, and the sentence expresses a complete thought. It is therefore indeed a sentence. It is also an independent clause.

Here is where the trouble starts, however. You might think that in order to remain an independent clause, the clause must stand on its own. But independent clauses can combine with other independent clauses. You just have to use the right punctuation to join them. And when you do not use the right punctuation, you risk writing a run-on sentence.

Consider these two independent clauses:

> Early Christians practiced communal sharing of resources.
> Their faith and community grew steadily.

If you were to join these sentences with no punctuation, it would look like this:

> Early Christians practiced communal sharing of resources their faith and community grew steadily.

Most readers would know how to interpret this sentence. In their minds, they would separate the first independent clause ("Early Christian communities") from the second ("their faith and community"). You make it easier on readers, though, if you separate—and rejoin—the sentences for them.

By convention, only certain combinations of punctuation and parts of speech can adequately join two independent clauses. A comma cannot do it by itself:

> Early Christians practiced communal sharing of resources, their faith and community grew steadily.

If you try to fuse two independent clauses with a comma, you create a run-on sentence. Indeed, most run-on sentences come from writers trying to join two independent clauses with a comma alone. It happens so often grammarians have invented a term for it: a comma splice. *Splice* simply means to join. A comma, however, is not strong enough to splice (or join) two independent clauses. If an architect tries to connect two freestanding towers with, say, a thin piece of bamboo, anyone who tries to walk from one tower to the other will invariably fall through. So, too, the architect of sentences. They need something stronger, some combination of punctuation and parts of speech, if they want to join their towers.

So, what *will* safely connect the freestanding towers of independent clauses and thereby avoid run-on sentences? You have several options.

1. **You can use a comma *and* a coordinating conjunction.**
   Do not let the term *coordinating conjunction* intimidate you. If you coordinate something, say an outfit, you match part to part, pants to shirt. And a conjunction simply means to connect or join two separate items. (Think of conjoined twins.) A coordinating conjunction therefore matches an independent clause to another independent clause with a word that connects the two. In grade school, you probably learned the acronym FANBOYS, which conveniently packages the most common coordinating conjunctions:

   For
   And
   Nor
   But
   Or
   Yet
   So

   Together with a comma, any of these words will adequately join two independent clauses. You just have to choose the right conjunction:

   Early Christians practiced communal sharing of resources**,** **and** their faith and community grew steadily.

   Or:

   Early Christians faced persecution for their beliefs**,** **but** their faith and community grew steadily.

2. **You can use a semicolon.**
   If the second independent clause follows logically from the first, you can join the independent clauses with a semicolon:

   Early Christians practiced communal sharing of resources**;** they aspired to live out the teachings of Jesus Christ as described in the New Testament.

This strategy only works if the first clause leads naturally to the second. In the sentence above, it does. In the following sentence, it does not:

> Early Christians faced persecution for their beliefs**;** their faith and community grew steadily.

This sentence is not a run-on sentence. But in fixing it, another problem has arisen: the second clause does not follow from the first. Why did their faith and community grow steadily as a result of persecution? A reader can guess. Maybe those who are persecuted tend to form or deepen their bonds? But readers should not have to guess. So...

3. **You can use a semicolon and a conjunctive adverb.**

Take another look at this sentence:

> Early Christians practiced communal sharing of resources**;** their faith and community grew steadily.

The sentence breaks down because the relationship between the two independent clauses is not obvious. You could, however, add a word that clarified the connection between the two clauses:

> Early Christians faced persecution for their beliefs**; however,** their faith and community grew steadily.

That word (*however*) is what is known as a conjunctive adverb. A conjunctive adverb allows you to establish a relationship between one independent clause and another. In addition to *however*, the most common conjunctive adverbs are *furthermore*, *moreover*, *nevertheless*, and *therefore*. Here is an example:

> Early Christian communities practiced communal sharing of resources**; therefore,** their faith and community grew steadily.

Notice the comma after *therefore*. If it were not there, the clause might confuse readers. You can see that even more clearly in this sentence:

> Early Christians faced persecution for their beliefs**; however** their faith and community grew steadily.

The second clause reads a little too much like a sentence fragment:

> However their faith and community grew steadily.

To which readers will ask, *However their faith and community grew steadily* what? A comma keeps readers from tripping over the second part of the sentence.

4. **You can use a period.**

To fix a run-on sentence, you can turn each independent clause into its own sentence. Using a period follows the same logic as using a semicolon. A period just adds a more definitive stop:

> Early Christian communities practiced communal sharing of resources. They aspired to live out the teachings of Jesus Christ as described in the New Testament.

As when you use a semicolon, sometimes you have to clarify the relationship between the two sentences. Here too you can choose from words like *however*, *nevertheless*, and so on.

> Early Christians faced persecution for their beliefs**.** **Nevertheless,** their faith and community grew steadily.

Because I prefer short (or shorter) sentences, I favor periods over semicolons. (Semicolons can also seem a little hoity-toity.) But you should definitely choose periods to join independent clauses when other clauses start to pile up. Take this run-on sentence:

> Early Christians faced persecution for their beliefs, often enduring hardships and martyrdom, their unwavering faith and sense of community not only endured but flourished, steadily expanding their influence and presence in the ancient world.

I could join these two independent clauses with a comma and a FANBOYS. Like so:

> Early Christians faced persecution for their beliefs, often enduring hardships and martyrdom, **but** their unwavering faith and sense of community not only endured but flourished, steadily expanding their influence and presence in the ancient world.

Or with a semicolon and a conjunctive adverb—that is, a word like *therefore* or *nevertheless*:

> Early Christians faced persecution for their beliefs, often enduring hardships and martyrdom**; however,** their unwavering faith and sense of community not only endured but flourished, steadily expanding their influence and presence in the ancient world.

But a period lets your reader take a breath before proceeding:

> Early Christians faced persecution for their beliefs, often enduring hardships and martyrdom**. However,** their

unwavering faith and sense of community not only endured but flourished, steadily expanding their influence and presence in the ancient world.

By the way, you may have heard that you should not begin a sentence with a coordinating conjunction like *And* or *But.* But that is nonsense. (Wink wink.) Feel free:

Early Christians faced persecution for their beliefs, often enduring hardships and martyrdom**. But** their unwavering faith and sense of community not only endured but flourished, steadily expanding their influence and presence in the ancient world.

5. **Finally, you can turn one of the independent clauses into a dependent clause.**

In this case, you would add a subordinating conjunction to the first independent clause and separate the two clauses with a comma. Now I will translate that into plain English. A subordinating clause, you will remember from the discussion of sentence fragments, is a clause that depends on the independent clause that follows it. Subordinating clauses begin with words like *although, because, if, since, whereas.* Simply add one of these words to the first independent clause and then lean it against the second one. Here too you have to make sure to choose the correct conjunction:

Because early Christians practiced communal sharing of resources, their faith and community grew steadily.

Or:

Although early Christians faced persecution for their beliefs**,** their faith and community grew steadily.

In addition to fixing run-on sentences, this strategy can create sentence variety. In the next chapter, I preach the virtues of short sentences. But the only thing worse than long sentences are sentences that are all the same length. Marrying a dependent clause to an independent one can create a long sentence and liven up your prose.

Pet Peeves

Before leaving the subject of run-on sentences, let me point out two related items. Elsewhere I have written that every teacher has their pet peeve—or, more often, pet peeves, plural. I may as well warn you of mine since other teachers may share them. Bear with me. These sentences raise the devil in me. Why? I could not say. I just know they do.

1. **You only need a comma if you are joining two independent clauses. If not, nix the comma.**

   So do not write this:

   > Early Christians faced persecution for their beliefs, but grew steadily.

   Grew steadily is not an independent clause. You may want the coordinating conjunction (*but*), but you do not need the comma. Instead, write this:

   > Early Christians faced persecution for their beliefs but grew steadily.

   To repeat, do not write this:

   > Early Christians practiced communal sharing of resources, and aspired to live out the teachings of Jesus Christ as described in the New Testament.

   Instead, write this:

   > Early Christians practiced communal sharing of resources and aspired to live out the teachings of Jesus Christ as described in the New Testament.

   No comma.

2. **If you join two independent clauses with a conjunctive adverb (*furthermore, however, moreover, nevertheless,* and *therefore*), you must (must!) use a semicolon (or a period) before it.**

   So, do not write this:

   > Early Christians faced persecution for their beliefs, however, their faith and community grew steadily.

   This sentence is still a run-on sentence. Indeed, the writer has only made it run on all the more by adding *however* without any additional punctuation. To fix it, you need a semicolon or period before *however*:

   > Early Christians faced persecution for their beliefs; however, their faith and community grew steadily.

   I think writers confuse this use of *however* with a different use of it:

   > Early Christians, however, faced persecution for their beliefs.

   In this sentence, *however* is not a conjunction. It does not join two things. Rather, it is an adverb. It modifies *faced.* Writers rarely add a semicolon to that sentence. But they often leave out a semicolon from a sentence like this one:

> Early Christian communities practiced communal sharing of resources, therefore, their faith and community grew steadily.

In doing so, they unwittingly take years off my life.

The Oxford Comma

> Who gives a fuck about an Oxford comma?
>
> —Vampire Weekend, "Oxford Comma"

I do! And you should too.

If the subject of run-on sentences concerns how to join parts of a sentence, the subject of Oxford commas concerns how to join items within a sentence. Before we wade into the arguments for or against it, what is an Oxford comma? Also known as a serial comma, an Oxford comma is the comma that comes before the conjunction in the next-to-last item in a list.[3] Here:

> The soldiers saluted the red, white, and blue.

The comma before *and* is the serial comma. Omit it, and the sentence would read like this:

> The soldiers saluted the red, white and blue.

Those who view the Oxford comma as unnecessary would point to the second sentence and argue that with all but a few exceptions, the serial comma clutters the page and wastes space. No one needs a comma between *white* and *and blue* to make sense of the sentence. Those who view the Oxford comma as necessary argue that space on a page is not particularly scarce. More to the point, while ninety-nine times out of one hundred the Oxford or serial comma is unnecessary, the one time a list needs it justifies its use in all other instances. In other words, it does more than just clutter up a page. It sometimes has a crucial job to do.

Grammarians like to have fun with examples illustrating what can go wrong when a writer omits a serial comma. Enjoy:

> The soldier recounted what he missed about being home: his dog, his little brother, the odor of his father's pipe and his girlfriend.

> Shown in this photo are Prince William, Prince George, Catherine holding her daughter and the Queen.
> We went for a walk with our dogs, grandma and grandpa.

In the first sentence, does the soldier miss his girlfriend or, like his father's pipe, her odor? In the second sentence, does Catherine hold the Queen too? Her lap is getting crowded. In the third, are the dogs named grandma and grandpa? Or did grandma and grandpa accompany the unnamed dogs on a walk?[4]

Grammarians invent such sentences to demonstrate the potential absurdities of excluding the serial comma. In the wild, though, few such sentences appear. That does not mean, however, that the lack of a serial comma never matters. Sometimes it matters a whole lot.

In 2018, a dairy company in Portland, Maine agreed to pay five million dollars to its truck drivers because a Maine law neglected to use a serial comma and thereby created a costly ambiguity. By law, workers in Maine, including truck drivers, receive time-and-a-half pay for each hour they work beyond forty in a week. However, the legislation carved out some exceptions to this law. Namely, that workers engaged in the following activities would not receive overtime pay:

> The canning, processing, preserving, freezing, drying, marketing, storing, packing for shipment or distribution of:
>
> 1. Agricultural produce;
> 2. Meat and fish products;
> 3. Perishable foods.

The lawsuit turned on whether the last item in the series ("packing for shipment or distribution of") involved one kind of work or two. If the law referred to one category of work and said that *only* workers who pack for shipment or distribution would not receive overtime pay, then truck drivers, who did not *pack* for shipment or distribution but merely *distributed,* should be eligible for overtime pay. If, by contrast, the last item referred to two separate kinds of work ("packing for shipment *or* distribution of"), then truck drivers, who distributed the products, should not, like all of the other workers engaged in the listed activities, be eligible for overtime pay.

The court ruled that since the law did not say whether the last item ("packing for shipment or distribution of") covered truck drivers or not, the drivers could claim the four years of overtime pay they had gone without, which, for this dairy, amounted to five million dollars. The state of Maine rewrote the law to clarify that those who distributed products—and not just those who packed them for shipment or distribution—were not eligible for overtime pay. In other words, they made it clear that the exception applied to truckers too. To accomplish this change, the Maine legislature inserted a comma—an Oxford comma—after shipment: "marketing, storing, packing for shipment, or distribution of...."[5]

Even when the stakes of a serial comma do not rise to five million dollars, they do have stakes. From time to time, the absence of a serial comma forces readers to puzzle out exactly what a writer means. *The New York Times* does not use Oxford commas, and, speaking as a reader of that paper, every couple of months I trip over one list or another and have to go back and figure out exactly what the sentence says. When I do, I get annoyed. You should never annoy your readers.

The lack of a serial comma can occasionally create ambiguity. The inclusion of it has never done so. Acting on the principle of better safe than sorry, most writers therefore favor its use. They do not go quite so far as Benjamin Dreyer, who argues that "only godless savages eschew the series comma."[6] But they, like me, believe that for the sake of clarity and consistency, writers should include it. Basically, it does no harm and, occasionally, some real good.

Exercises

1. Write a paragraph (three to five sentences) on any of the following topics:
   A. Should college be free?
   B. Should college students have to take general education classes outside their major? Or should they simply focus on the classes that will prepare them for their chosen career?
   C. In the United States, a president can win an election not by winning the most votes but by winning the most electoral votes. (Electoral votes are assigned to states by adding up their representatives and senators. For example, California has fifty-five, while Montana has three. There are 538 total electoral votes.) Does this system assure that smaller states still matter? Or does it violate the principle of direct democracy—that is, whoever wins the most votes should win an election?

   Once you have written your paragraph, turn each sentence into a fragment or a run-on.

2. Here are twelve sentence fragments. Diagnose what each lacks (subject, verb, complete thought, or all three), and then add what it needs to make it a bona fide sentence.
   A. In *The Fire Next Time*, James Baldwin vividly illustrating the urgency of racial equality.
   B. In *The Fire Next Time*, vividly illustrates the urgency of racial equality.
   C. Although in *The Fire Next Time* James Baldwin vividly illustrates the urgency of racial equality.
   D. In *The Fire Next Time*, vividly illustrating the urgency of racial equality.
   E. Free will, a concept central to philosophy and theology, raising fundamental questions about human agency and the nature of existence.
   F. A concept central to philosophy and theology, raises fundamental questions about human agency and the nature of existence.
   G. A concept central to philosophy and theology, raising fundamental questions about human agency and the nature of existence.
   H. Raising fundamental questions about human agency and the nature of existence.
   I. The discriminatory practice that systematically denied loans and services to people in certain neighborhoods based on race, redlining continuing to have lasting effects on housing patterns and wealth disparities in the United States.
   J. The discriminatory practice that systematically denied loans and services to people in certain neighborhoods based on race, continues to have lasting effects on housing patterns and wealth disparities in the United States.
   K. The discriminatory practice that systematically denied loans and services to people in certain neighborhoods based on race, continuing to have lasting effects on housing patterns and wealth disparities in the United States.
   L. While redlining, the discriminatory practice that systematically denied loans and services to people in certain neighborhoods based on race, continues to have lasting effects on housing patterns and wealth disparities in the United States.

3. Here are three run-on sentences about cave painting. Fix each sentence four different ways: (1) add a comma and coordinating conjunction (FANBOYS); (2) insert a semicolon with or without a conjunctive adverb (*furthermore, however, moreover, nevertheless*, and *therefore*); (3) use a period to break the independent clauses into two sentences. You may need to add a conjunctive adverb: *furthermore, however, moreover, nevertheless*, and *therefore*; (4) add a subordinating conjunction (*although, because, if, since, unless, whereas, while*) and turn one of the clauses into a dependent clause.
   A. Cave painting dates back tens of thousands of years, it is one of the earliest forms of human artistic expression.
   B. These paintings were created with supposedly crude techniques like finger painting, blowing pigment through tubes, and using brushes made from animal hair, they depict a wide range of subjects such as animals, human figures, abstract symbols, and scenes of daily life.
   C. Archaeologists admire cave paintings for their aesthetic value, they offer valuable insights into the beliefs, practices, and environments of early humans.

4. Do you need a comma in any of the following sentences? Why or why not? Add one, take one out, or do nothing.
   A. Disparities in access to quality education contribute to persistent gaps in academic achievement, and opportunities for students from marginalized communities.
   B. Deregulation reduced government intervention in the airline industry and led to increased competition, lower prices for consumers and greater innovation.
   C. Magical thinking may seem irrational but it often serves as a coping mechanism or a way to find meaning in the world.
   D. In 1848, Phineas Gage survived an explosion that sent an iron rod through his skull but the accident dramatically changed his personality.
   E. Terrorism remains a global threat, and instills fear across nations.

5. The paragraphs below contain at least one of each of the following errors: (1) a comma splice; (2) a missing Oxford comma; (3) a needless comma; (4) a run-on sentence; and (5) a sentence

fragment. Find the errors and revise the paragraph. Here is a hint: except for the first sentence of the first paragraph, there is one error in every sentence.

Abolitionism, a transformative social and political movement, emerged in the eighteenth century with the goal of eradicating the institution of slavery. Rooted in the principles of human rights and equality, arguing vehemently against the dehumanizing practice of slavery, and advocating for the immediate emancipation of enslaved individuals. Central to the abolitionist movement was the belief that slavery was morally wrong, and fundamentally incompatible with the values of a just and humane society.

Abolitionists employed a variety of tactics to advance their cause, including public lectures, composing anti-slavery literature, organizing boycotts and participating in direct action such as the Underground Railroad, a network of secret routes and safe houses that helped enslaved individuals escape to freedom. Key figures in the abolitionist movement, such as Frederick Douglass, Harriet Tubman, and William Lloyd Garrison, played instrumental roles in raising awareness about the brutal realities of slavery, they galvanized public support for its abolition.

Abolitionists faced staunch opposition from pro-slavery interests, particularly in the Southern United States where the economy depended heavily on slave labor, however, they remained steadfast in their commitment to their cause. Although their efforts bore fruit with the abolition of slavery in many countries, including the United States with the ratification of the 13th Amendment in 1865. The abolitionist movement stands as a testament to the power of activism and it illustrates the power of activism to effect lasting change.

CHAPTER 7

The Long and Short of It: On Sentence Variety

Like the occasional sentence it asks you to write, this chapter is short. Start by considering this paragraph on pop music that ChatGPT kindly generated for me:

> Pop music, a genre characterized by catchy melodies and broad appeal, has been a dominant force in the music industry for decades. Its origins date back to the mid-20th century, gaining popularity with artists like Elvis Presley and The Beatles. Pop music is known for its diverse range of styles, from upbeat dance tracks to heartfelt ballads. This versatility has allowed it to resonate with a wide and diverse audience, making it a universal language in the world of music. Contemporary pop artists continue to shape and redefine the genre, blending influences from various musical traditions to create chart-topping hits that capture the essence of the times.

The paragraph commits none or few of the errors I warn against in this book. Sure, by using a more interesting verb in the first sentence, it might shed some unnecessary words:

> Pop music, a genre characterized by catchy melodies and broad appeal, has ~~been a dominant force in~~ **dominated** the music industry for decades.

And "chart-topping hits" seems a little redundant. Could a hit *not* top the charts? And could a song that tops the charts *not* be a hit? And some might argue that "the essence of the times" is a cliché.

For the most part, however, the paragraph is fine. Except for one thing, which is that it is heavy dull. At best, your mind starts to wander. At worst, the paragraph rocks you to sleep.

It does so for several reasons, but one of the most obvious is that the sentences sound too much alike. Each is a declarative sentence marching lockstep to a subject-verb-object beat:

> Pop music...has been a dominant force...
> Its origins date back to the mid-20th century...
> Pop music is known for its diverse range of styles...
> This versatility has allowed it...
> Contemporary pop artists continue to shape and redefine the genre...

A does B, C does D, E does F, and so on. If you want to learn how to make something as lively as pop music sound as lifeless as possible, take notes.

Sentence *structure* explains much of the tranquilizing effect of this paragraph, but a larger share belongs to sentence *length*. I did not ask ChatGTP to generate just any paragraph on pop music. I asked it to generate a paragraph on pop music that had roughly the same number of words in each sentence. ChatGTP complied. Here is the word count:

> Sentence one: 22 words
> Sentence two: 18 words
> Sentence three: 17 words
> Sentence four: 23 words
> Sentence five: 27 words

The average is 21.4 words per sentence. The range is 17 to 27 words. In other words, barely any range at all. The fix for this uniformity should be obvious: compose sentences that have a wider spread of word counts. In *The Portrait of a Lady*, the novelist Henry James includes a sentence that is 207 words long. (It contains two colons!) But you and I are not Henry James. Nor are our readers Henry James's readers. The longer the sentence, the more likely it spins out of our control, and the more trouble readers will have holding on as it spins out of control.

If long sentences carry risks to writer and reader alike, the solution should be to compose shorter—and occasionally quite short—sentences. For whatever reason, though, many writers hesitate to compose short sentences. Instead, their prose is far more likely to look like the neither-long-nor-short sentences on pop music generated by ChatGTP. Why? My hunch is that writers associate short sentences with simplemindedness and long sentences with complexity. Children learn how to read from books that have deliberately short sentences: "Goodnight, Moon." "He was a big fat caterpillar." "Down fell the snow—plop!—on top of Peter's head." If short sentences are for children, the logic goes, then long sentences must be for adults.

But short does not necessarily mean simple—or, better said, simpleminded. Microsoft Word offers this wonderful though little-known feature called Editor. Among other statistics, it calculates the average length of sentences in a document. My chapter on clichés, for example, has 15.1 words per sentence. That is roughly six words fewer per sentence than the paragraph about pop music quoted above. Yet I hope no one thinks my chapter on clichés is simple or simpleminded. It is, after all, trying to persuade writers that they have more options when it comes to clichés than simply following the shopworn advice of deleting them.

So, if you want to break up the monotony of your sentences, insert shorter ones. How can you do that? One strategy is to do what I did in the sentence right before this one, which is to ask a question. ("How can you do that?") Questions are usually short, but they have the additional advantage of departing from the pattern of declarative sentence after declarative sentence that characterizes most writing. (Exclamations do too!) For an even more extreme version of the question strategy, glance at the paragraph above that begins "If long sentences carry risks to writer and reader alike...." Midway through that paragraph, speculating about writers preferring long sentences to short ones, I write a one-word sentence in the form of a question: "Why?" Sentences do not come much shorter than that.

But not all types of writing invite questions. A paragraph explaining the 1924 Immigration Act, for example, might look strange if you stopped to ask and answer a question. But you do not need to pose questions to write short sentences. Far from it. The previous sentence ("Far from it") has all of three words. You will sometimes see writers use this short-sentence strategy after they outline an argument that they then go on to question. The approach works best if the previous sentence is long and somewhat complex. For example:

> The conventional wisdom about the relationship between interest rates and the stock market is that as central banks raise interest rates in an effort to combat inflation, the cost of borrowing increases, leading to reduced corporate spending and consumer demand, which, in turn, causes stock market volatility as investors reassess the growth potential of companies across various sectors,

> often shifting their portfolios toward more conservative, fixed-income securities. So far so good. But the conventional wisdom ignores....

The "So far so good" saves your reader from drowning in the details of the previous sentence. It also signals that readers should prepare themselves for you to question the claim you just summarized.

But short sentences do not have to be three words long. Recall the advice I offered in chapter six about run-on sentences. One way to write shorter sentences is to break up existing sentences that go on longer than they probably should. Look again at the above paragraph. If you wanted to make it easier on readers, you could break the first sentence into three shorter ones.

> The conventional wisdom about the relationship between interest rates and the stock market is that as central banks raise interest rates in an effort to combat inflation, the cost of borrowing increases. **The increased cost of borrowing leads** ~~leading~~ to reduced corporate spending and consumer demand, which, in turn, causes stock market volatility as investors reassess the growth potential of companies across various sectors. **Investors often respond by** shifting their portfolios toward more conservative, fixed-income securities. So far so good. But the conventional wisdom ignores....

The same advice about breaking long sentences into shorter ones applies to sentences that prop dependent clauses onto independent ones. Take this sentence:

> Although the blues emerged from the hardships of African American life in the early twentieth century, it quickly became a powerful form of artistic expression that resonated with people from all walks of life.

Except for the cliché ("all walks of life") and the uninspired linking verb ("became"), that sentence is fine. If need be, however, you could break it into two shorter sentences:

> **The** blues emerged from the hardships of African American life in the early twentieth century**. Yet** it quickly became a powerful form of artistic expression that resonated with people from all walks of life.

Too many sentences like these—shorter but not too short—would read as badly as too many neither short-nor-long sentences. But shorter-but-not-too-short sentences can also provide variety. And that is what matters.

However you manage it, varying sentence length, especially if you include shorter sentences, will do at least two things for your prose. One, short sentences keep your reader awake. They let them take a breath mid-paragraph, which restores them for the sentences that follow. Two, as a rule, the shorter the sentence, the more readable it is. The Editor function in MS Word includes another feature that estimates what grade level a reader would have to complete to be able to understand what you have written. It does so by calculating the number of words per sentence and the number of characters per sentence—that is, longer sentences composed of longer words tend to make reading more difficult and vice versa. (I take up the latter issue in the next chapter on pretentious diction.) I am proud to report that someone in seventh grade could read my chapter on clichés and follow along. To make sense of the paragraph about pop music at the start of this chapter, however, a reader would need to be a senior in high school. And the paragraph about the relationship between interest rates and the stock market? A reader would need to be in the thirty-third grade to understand it. Since that grade does not exist, you can infer how many people could understand the sentence. Very few indeed.

The upshot is to write Goldilocks sentences, neither too long nor too short, broken up by the occasional short sentence or two. Trust me.

Exercises

1. Take the paragraph below on the Immigration Act of 1924 and vary the sentence lengths. Insert a question. Write a very short sentence. Turn a long sentence into two or three shorter ones. Recast a sentence with a dependent and an independent clause into two separate sentences. Overall, see if you can reduce the average number of words per sentence to fifteen or fewer, which should, in theory, also increase the spread of the number of words in each sentence. As it stands, the average is 28.2.

   While the Chinese Exclusion Act of 1882 marked the beginning of racially discriminatory immigration policies in the United States, the 1924 Immigration Act, also known as the Johnson-Reed Act, expanded these restrictions by establishing quotas that severely limited immigration from Asia and other non-European regions. It represents a pivotal moment in US immigration policy, profoundly shaping the demographic landscape of the nation. Enacted against the backdrop of nativist sentiments and xenophobia, the legislation sought to curb the influx of immigrants, particularly from Southern and Eastern European countries. By establishing quotas based on national origins, the law restricted the number of immigrants from each country to a percentage of their presence in the US population according to the 1890 census, thereby favoring immigrants from Northern and Western European countries.

This deliberate preference for certain ethnic and regional groups reflected a desire to maintain a racial and ethnic homogeneity and curb the perceived threats associated with cultural diversity. Additionally, the act virtually banned immigration from Asia, exemplifying a broader trend of discriminatory immigration policies during this period. The Immigration Act of 1924 left an enduring impact on US immigration patterns, shaping the composition of the population for decades to come.

2. Type the first paragraph from the passage on the Immigration Act into Microsoft Word and find out what grade a reader would need to have completed in order to understand it. See if your revision can cut the grade level in half. If not, keep revising.

3. What subject do you know more about than most of your friends or family? Backgammon? Basketball? Birdwatching? Write a paragraph (approximately three to five sentences) explaining what makes your pastime great. Make each sentence between twenty and thirty words long.

4. Take the paragraph you wrote for exercise three and reduce the average rate of words per sentence to no more than fifteen. To reach that number, you will need to compose several short sentences and at least one very, very short sentence.

5. What grade level did your original paragraph in exercise three require of a reader? And your revised paragraph?

6. Read through something you wrote at another time or for another class. Find a paragraph in which all the sentences are more or less the same length. Break a long sentence into two shorter ones and insert a very short sentence.

CHAPTER 8

Pretentious Diction: On the Sesquipedalian

> Do not be tempted by a twenty-dollar word when there is a ten-center handy, ready and able. Anglo-Saxon is a livelier tongue than Latin, so use Anglo-Saxon words.[1]
>
> —E. B. White, *The Elements of Style*

Think about what you have learned about style so far. Where does this sentence go wrong:

> In order to adapt to changing market dynamics, the company decided to commence a strategic rebranding initiative, eventually launching an invigorated new logo that promised to connect with the fluctuating tastes of consumers.

Above all, the sentence is wordy: "adapt to changing market dynamics" and "decided to commence a strategic rebranding initiative" stand out the most. If you have to *adapt* to something, like the market, you can safely assume it is changing. If something has *dynamics*, it too is probably changing. And as an economist would point out, *markets*, by definition, change. You could probably do away with both of the adjectives, "changing" and "dynamic," but keep one just to be safe. As for "decided to commence a strategic rebranding initiative," if you *commence* something, like a rebranding initiative, you must have already *decided* to do so. So "decided" can go.

I might be tempted to cut "strategic" too. Would a company commence an *arbitrary* rebranding initiative? For that matter, what is the difference between *rebranding* and a "rebranding initiative"? But I will let those last two pass. I cannot, however, spare "In order to." You can almost always substitute *to* for *in order to*. All told, you could rewrite the sentence like this:

> To adapt to market dynamics, the company commenced a strategic rebranding initiative, eventually launching an invigorated new logo that promised to connect with the fluctuating tastes of consumers.

That is better, but it still sounds off. Why? Because the sentence suffers from another problem, which is pretentious diction or, less formally, too many fancy words. Instead of saying *commence*, the sentence could just say *begin*. Instead of saying *invigorated*, it could just say *lively*. And instead of saying *fluctuating*, it could just say *changing*. So why did the writer choose *commenced*, *invigorated*, and *fluctuating*? Since the author is ChatGPT, we cannot ask it. But the answer is clear enough. The writers who constitute the collective internet unconscious that ChatGPT scrapes for its answers wanted to sound smart, and they thought *commence* sounded smarter than *begin*, *invigorated* smarter than *lively*, and *fluctuating* smarter than *changing*. The question is why: why these writers wanted to sound smart and why *commence*, *invigorated*, and *fluctuating* sounded smart to them.

I blame the French.

In 1066, the Duke of Normandy took advantage of a succession crisis and invaded England. His invasion displaced Harold II, king of the Germanic settlers, collectively known as the Anglo-Saxons, who had occupied Britain after the Roman army left the country in 410 CE. Historians refer to the invasion by the Duke of Normandy as the Norman Conquest. As conquests tend to do, it profoundly changed the conquered country, not least its language. Prior to the Norman Conquest, the inhabitants of Britain spoke Old English, which derived from the Germanic languages the Anglo-Saxons carried with them to the island. After 1066, the Normans brought their own language (or, more accurately, languages) with them. The Normans spoke a French dialect, much of which derived from Latin.[2] They also conducted their legal, religious, and academic business in straight-up Latin. In the centuries after 1066, one language did not win out over the other so much as all fell into an uneasy coexistence.

That history explains why English has so many words that mean more or less the same thing. For example, Anglo-Saxons would have used the word *light*; the Normans would have used the word *illuminate*. Following the Anglo-Saxons, you can say, "the candle lit the room." Or if you prefer

Latin via French, you can say, "the candle illuminated the room." Indeed, my dictionary uses *illuminate* to define the word *light*, and vice versa.

The words may be synonyms; however, they are not equals. The Norman elite spoke the Latin-inflected French dialect they brought with them. By contrast, the common people spoke Anglo-Saxon. This class divide still exists. To our ears, Latin-derived words sound more sophisticated than Anglo-Saxon ones. So, the logic goes, if you want to sound sophisticated (and who does not want to sound sophisticated?), you say *illuminate* instead of *light*. Or *initiate* instead of *start*. Or *inquire* instead of *ask*. Or *commence* instead of *begin*. Or, and this one grates on my ears more than others, perhaps because students love to use it so very much, *plethora*. For example, "the archive contains a plethora of books on nineteenth-century working-class literature written by women." More often than not, *many* works just fine. I will also accept *an abundance*.

The preference for the Latin over the Anglo-Saxon explains how you get sentences like this one:

> Shakespeare's enduring literary legacy resides not only in the lyrical cadence of his verse but also in the kaleidoscopic profundity with which he navigated the human condition, rendering his works an inexhaustible wellspring of insight into the complexities of existence.

With the exception of "wellspring," which combines two Anglo-Saxon words, each of the major words in this sentence has Latin roots. Writers might think this sentence makes them sound smart, but in reality, it just makes them sound pompous. Imagine how ridiculous it would sound if, before a NASCAR race began, the announcer intoned, "Drivers, commence your engines!" The Shakespeare sentence sounds like that.

To return to our original sentence about rebranding, what words you choose will affect how your reader imagines you as a writer. Do you aspire to join the elite? Or are you comfortable with the plain? Recall our first pass at a revision:

> To adapt to **market dynamics**, the company **commenced** a strategic rebranding initiative, eventually launching an **invigorated** new logo that promised to connect with the **fluctuating** tastes of consumers.

Here is another revision without the fancy words:

> To adapt to a changing market, the company **began** a strategic rebranding initiative, eventually launching a **lively** new logo that promised to connect with **shifting** consumer tastes.

The new version sacrifices some sophistication, but the purpose of writing is not to sound sophisticated. It is to communicate with readers as clearly, concisely, and persuasively as possible. You should therefore try to eliminate whatever gets in the way of that purpose, including words you think make you sound smart but that readers will easily see through.

George Orwell referred to words such as *commence*, *invigorated*, and *fluctuating* as pretentious diction. Pretentious diction almost always involves words derived from Latin. That is why in his famous essay "Politics and the English Language," Orwell complains that

> [b]ad writers, and especially scientific, political and sociological writers, are nearly always haunted by the notion that Latin or Greek words are grander than Saxon ones, and unnecessary words like *expedite*, *ameliorate*, *predict*, *extraneous*, *deracinated*, *clandestine*, *sub-aqueous* and hundreds of others constantly gain ground from their Anglo-Saxon opposite numbers.

The menace of pretentious diction also explains why E. B. White, whose *The Elements of Style* is the grandfather of style guides, advises writers to use Anglo-Saxon words instead of Latin ones.

That is good advice as far as it goes. But there is a problem. Most writers do not know which words come from Latin and which from Anglo-Saxon. To be sure, longer, more complicated words—like *legacy*, *cadence*, or *profundity*—almost always come from Latin. But the reverse—shorter, plainer words almost always coming from Anglo-Saxon—is not necessarily true. Even if writers did know which words came from where, the distinction would not always serve them well.

Consider a word like *pusillanimous*. My dictionary defines it as showing a lack of courage or determination. Only a writer out to impress their reader would use a word like *pusillanimous*. The Cowardly Lion, from *The Wizard of Oz*, would sound silly if the author of the book, L. Frank Baum, had called his creation the Pusillanimous Lion. So, what word should a writer use instead? They could follow Baum in using *cowardly*. But *cowardly* derives from the Latin word *cauda*, or tail. (No one knows why, but the assumption is that *cauda* and thus *coward* refer to how a frightened animal would run away with its tail between its legs.) Ruling out *cowardly* because of its Latin origins, perhaps we could use *timid.* The Timid Lion. Oops. *Timid* also derives from Latin: *timere,* to fear. I suppose you could go with *fearful,* an Anglo-Saxon word, but is the Fearful Lion demonstrably better than the Cowardly Lion? Not that I can see. In which case, why should anyone care about where a word comes from?

Instead of categorically preferring Anglo-Saxon words to Latin ones, we need another rule to guide us in our word choices. In honor of E. B. White, call it the ten-cent rule. Do not be tempted by twenty-dollar words like *pusillanimous* or *commence* when ten-cent words like *cowardly* or *begin* cost much less and convey much more, regardless of where they come from. Orwell offered similar advice. He wanted writers to use "the fewest and shortest words that will cover one's meaning," regardless of whether peasants or pedants used them. The lion should be *cowardly,* even if *cowardly* is a Latin and not an Anglo-Saxon word. The obligation is to choose the best word—not the word with the most appropriate pedigree.[3]

Sesquipedalian Diction

Yet the rule to use ten-cent words instead of twenty-dollar ones should not be taken as gospel. In the chapter on clichés, I refer to H. W. Fowler as "the crankiest of perhaps all style docents." I could have used the word *guide* instead of *docent.* The words mean about the same thing, and *guide* is the more familiar and, thus, easier word for a reader. But, to invoke Orwell, *guide* would not cover my meaning. A *guide* can lead you down a forest path or describe the city from a cramped, overheated tour bus. By contrast, a *docent* works in museums and art galleries. If I had to follow the ten-cent rule, I would have to use *guide.* But *docent* is closer to the truth. H. W. Fowler wore tweed suits, smoked a pipe, and had rigorous rules about English usage. He is not a guide. He is a docent.

In sum, a writer has to choose which word fits best, keeping in mind that a lot of things (origin, familiarity, accuracy) will dictate which word fits best.

That said, you can, and perhaps should, leave a little room in your heart—and in your writing—for the twenty-dollar words. As I wrote this chapter, I was reading a novel that in the middle of its otherwise plainspoken prose dropped the word "borborygmus" onto the page. Borborygmus! Who knew English had such an astonishing word like borborygmus? It means "a rumbling or gurgling noise made by the movement of fluid and gas in the intestines." Orwell, White, and pretty much every author of style books would probably tell you to stay away from a word like *borborygmus.* Instead, they would recommend *rumbling* or *gurgling.* I disagree. I believe writers can get away with an occasional *borborygmus*—or even *pusillanimous*—so long as it is the only twenty-dollar word they deposit in a piece of writing.

To write well, you have to love words. All words. You can communicate that love by using the clearest, plainest, and least pretentious language you can. You can also communicate it by occasionally using a delightfully arcane word like *defenestrate*. (It means to throw someone out of a window.) Or *milquetoast*, which means a timid person or, as an adjective, lifeless. (For example, a *milquetoast* speech on a controversial topic.) Or why not *sesquipedalian*, which, appropriately, means characterized by long words? Used indiscriminately, these words mark the writer as pretentious. Used sparingly, they mark the writer as someone who loves the taste and shape of words and who can, perhaps, inspire a similar love in readers. By falling for them, writers may not necessarily succumb to temptation but, rather, to joy.

These words come with one more advantage. Throughout this book, I keep an eye out for ways that writers can distinguish their prose from the milquetoast prose generated by artificial intelligence. Among other strategies, the writer can include the occasional fancy word. Unless prompted, artificial intelligence will never use a word like *sesquipedalian*. First, that word does not appear often enough in the archive of internet prose for ChatGPT or other artificial intelligence language programs to use it. Second, ChatGPT and other large language systems do not love words enough—they do not love anything—to cherish a word like *sesquipedalian*. Or *defenestrate*. Or *milquetoast*. But human writers can love words. Indeed, I would argue that to write well, they have to love words.

Sucks

If the occasional fancy word can distinguish your writing from that produced by artificial intelligence, so too can the occasional demotic word. (*Demotic* does not have a good synonym. It means ordinary, popular.) Consider this sentence I recently came across in a book review about, appropriately enough, artificial intelligence: "Much of the current discourse about artificial intelligence sucks."[4] This sentence goes from the highly formal ("current discourse about artificial intelligence") to the highly informal ("sucks"). The contrast is jarring but delightful.

Here is another example, this one from an article about whether or not a president should enjoy immunity for crimes committed while they were in office. If they do, the argument runs, then a president could, hypothetically, order the assassination of a political rival. "This is," the journalist writes, "as the nation's founders would certainly agree, completely bonkers."[5] Up to that point in the article, the writer has used not quite dry but at least formal English. And then we get "completely bonkers." The phrase works even better because it is associated with the founding fathers, who, in their breeches and white wigs, suddenly agree to a word like *bonkers*.

Again, unless you tell it to, ChatGPT is as bad at drawing on lively words like *sucks* and *bonkers* as it is at drawing on fancy words like *salubrious* or *resplendent*. (It also has no use for slang.) Its ignorance of lively and fancy words alike leaves room for the human writer to write something only a human could. In so doing, it gives readers yet another reason to prefer human writers to artificial ones.

Exercises

1. Etymology refers to "the origin of a word and the historical development of its meaning." For example, the word *day* derives from the Old English word *daeg*. By contrast, the word *transgress* traveled from Latin via French to English. It means "to go beyond the bounds of (a moral principle or other established standard of behavior)." It is composed of two Latin words: *trans-* and *gradi-*. *Trans* meant "across" and *gradi-* meant "go" or "step." Thus, *transgress* means to go (or step) across. In a good dictionary, look up the etymology of the words below. Which come from Anglo-Saxon? Which from Latin?
   A. Bold
   B. Cognition
   C. Earth
   D. Evil
   E. House
   F. Jurisdiction
   G. Nominate
   H. Old
   I. Rejuvenate
   J. Spectacle
   K. Wonder
   L. Work

2. Take the Latin words from Exercise One and break them into their component parts. What other English words do their parts form? For example, add *pro-* (forward) to the root *gradi-* or *gress-* in *transgress* and you get *progress*: to step or go forward.

3. Find synonyms for these possibly pretentious words. If you cannot find a one-to-one match, you can use two simpler words. For example, the first draft of this chapter used the word *egregious* to describe two particularly wordy patches of prose. Worrying that *egregious* crossed the line into the pretentious, I substituted *stand out.*
   A. Cacophonous
   B. Confabulate
   C. Concupiscence
   D. Ebullient
   E. Ineffable
   F. Genuflect
   G. Lugubrious
   H. Mellifluous
   I. Noetic
   J. Obfuscate
   K. Perambulate
   L. Perspicacious
   M. Prolixity
   N. Quixotic
   O. Redolent
   P. Sclerotic
   Q. Supercilious

4. Fix this only slightly exaggerated ChatGPT-generated sentence. Feel free to cut words rather than replace them.

   In the multifarious dance of finance, astute individuals employ a judicious amalgam of research, prudence, and malleability to navigate through the intricacies of markets, ensuring their financial endeavors are not merely transactions but proficient strategies for durable success.

5. Do you have a favorite from the list of pretentious words in Exercise Three? Use it in a sentence.

6. This sentence came straight out of the mouth of the ChatGPT babe. Fix it. Trim the wordiness while you are at it.

   Frida Kahlo, the illustrious Mexican surrealist, transcends mere artistic paradigms, encapsulating a profound fusion of poignant introspection and visceral symbolism within the intricate tapestry of her oeuvre, thereby rendering her a luminary provocateur of avant-garde expression.

7. Write three to five sentences on the dangers associated with one of these four topics:
   A. The Electoral College
   B. Gambling on Professional Sports
   C. Social Media
   D. Climate Change

   Make your sentences relatively formal but at some point, incorporate an informal word like *sucks* or *bonkers*.

8. Read through something you wrote at another time or for another class. Do you see any words that suggest you were trying to sound smart? Underline them and replace them with a simpler or more appropriate word.

CHAPTER 9

Conventions

In college, I briefly studied in France. As a newcomer to the country, I quickly learned two lessons. First, unlike in the United States, the French will stand up and lean against a bar to drink a glass of beer or wine. You sometimes see this done in the United States, but usually out of necessity—all the seats at the bar are taken—rather than habit. Second, again unlike in the United States, the French do not tip servers and bartenders or, if they do, they leave a token amount, like rounding up the bill to the nearest whole number. Instead, the tip, so called, is already reflected in the bill. (If you look at a receipt, you will see an item labeled *service compris* or "service included.") I discovered *service compris* the hard way. I drank a beer (standing) and left behind a twenty percent tip. The barkeep ran me down outside the bar to give me the money he assumed I had mistakenly left behind. Lesson learned.

These practices—sitting or standing, tipping or not tipping—are known as conventions. A convention is what is usually done. Different countries, even different regions of a country, have different conventions. Some cultures value punctuality more than others. Others have more or less formal ways for people to greet each other. And no one can seem to agree on what time to eat dinner.

I mention these conventions because in what follows I describe how writers and editors have decided to present certain information like numbers, titles, and quotations. Most style guides refer to these practices as mechanics, which, like conventions, means how things are done. (A synonym for mechanics would be *the ins and outs*. For example, *the mechanics of day trading*.) I prefer the term *conventions*, though, because often there is no good reason to do something one way rather than another. We have simply agreed—or not—on how to do it. For instance, if you live in England, you put a period after quotation marks, like so: "All men are created equal". Yet in the United States, the period goes before the quotation marks: "All men are created equal." Is one way better than the other? Not that I can see.

Nevertheless, as the proverb goes, when in Rome, do as the Romans do. While some of the rules that follow may seem arbitrary, readers have learned to expect them. Therefore, writers would do well to follow them. The rules below do not cover everything. Instead, they cover the issues that arise most often in student writing. The rules for numbers and titles follow Chicago style. The rules for quotations follow MLA style. Also, to make these guidelines more usable, I have simplified some rules and, in the section on quotations, left some abstruse parts out. For these, students should consult a more thorough guide.

Numbers

1. **Spell out numbers up to 100.**
   Among the participants, ~~12~~ **twelve** individuals belonged to the lower-income bracket.

2. **Use hyphens for numbers with two words.**
   The survey indicated that ~~forty two~~ **forty-two** households out of fifty had access to high-speed internet.

3. **Use numerals for numbers greater than 100.**
   The national census data revealed that ~~fifteen hundred and fifty~~ **1,550** households experienced economic displacement due to gentrification in the metropolitan area.

4. **If a sentence starts with a number, spell out the number.**
   ~~80~~ **Eighty** individuals out of the 100 surveyed voted in the last election.

5. **Use numerals to cite page numbers.**
   In *The Fire Next Time,* James Baldwin writes, "People who imagine that history flatters them (as it does, indeed, since they wrote it) are impaled on their history like a butterfly on a pin and become incapable of seeing or changing themselves or the world" (~~ninety-five~~ **95**).

6. **Spell out percentages (unless the percentage includes a decimal).**
   The top ~~10~~ **ten** percent of earners in the United States control a disproportionately large share of the nation's wealth.

7. **Spell out *percent*.**
   According to recent polling data, sixty-two~~%~~ **percent** of voters support the proposed policy change on healthcare reform.

8. **Do not use an apostrophe after a decade.**
   The ~~1920's~~ **1920s** was a decade marked by significant experimentation and innovation in literature.

9. **Spell out centuries.**
   The ~~19th~~ **nineteenth** century witnessed a flourishing of literary works characterized by a focus on emotion, nature, and individualism.

10. **When used as nouns, centuries do *not* need hyphens.**
    Many literary works of the ~~twentieth-century~~ **twentieth century** grappled with the effects of global conflicts.

11. **When used as adjectives, centuries *do* need hyphens.**
    ~~Nineteenth century~~ **Nineteenth-century** literature witnessed a flourishing of works characterized by a focus on emotion, nature, and individualism.

Titles

1. **Place the titles of short stories, poems, and essays within quotation marks.**
   In ~~*Bartleby, the Scrivener,*~~ **"Bartleby, the Scrivener,"** which appears in the collection *The Piazza Tales*, Herman Melville explores themes of alienation and the human condition through the character of Bartleby, whose passive resistance challenges societal norms.

2. **Place almost everything else (books, magazines, newspapers, pamphlets, long poems, plays) in italics.**
   In ~~"The Hunger Games,"~~ ***The Hunger Games,*** Suzanne Collins uses a dystopian setting to explore themes of power, survival, and the impact of violence on youth.

3. **In titles, capitalize nouns, pronouns, verbs, adjectives, and adverbs. Do not capitalize articles (a, an, the), coordinating conjunctions (for, and, nor, but, or, yet, so), or prepositions (of, in, to). A decent rule of thumb is not to capitalize words that are three or fewer letters.**
   The Old Man ~~And The~~ ***and the*** *Sea.*

Quotations

The examples below draw from the opening paragraph of Toni Morrison's *Beloved*:

> 124 was spiteful. Full of a baby's venom. The women in the house knew it and so did the children. For years each put up with the spite in his own way, but by 1873 Sethe and her daughter Denver were its only victims. The grandmother, Baby Suggs, was dead, and the sons, Howard and Buglar, had run away by the time they were thirteen years old—as soon as merely looking in a mirror shattered it (that was the signal for Buglar); as soon as two tiny hand prints appeared in the cake (that was it for Howard). Neither boy waited to see more; another kettleful of chickpeas smoking in a heap on the floor; soda crackers crumbled and strewn in a line next to the doorsill. Nor did they wait for one of the relief periods: the weeks, months even, when nothing was disturbed. No. Each one fled at once—the moment the house committed what was for him the one insult not to be borne or witnessed a second time around.[1]

In my edition of the novel, the passage appears on page three.

1. **Discuss works of literature in the present tense.**
   Beloved ~~began~~ **begins** with these haunting words: "124 was spiteful. Full of a baby's venom. The women in the house knew it and so did the children."

For other works, consider the context. If you refer to something ongoing, use the present tense. If you refer to something that happened in the past, use the past tense.
The 13th Amendment to the United States Constitution **abolishes** slavery and involuntary servitude, except as punishment for a crime.

The 13th Amendment to the United States Constitution, ratified in 1865, **abolished** slavery and involuntary servitude, except as punishment for a crime.

2. **Do not just drop a quotation into your prose. Introduce it with a signal phrase like *As Morrison observes* or *As Morrison writes*. Signal phrases announce to your reader, "Here comes a quotation!"**
Beloved does not start with what is happening now but with what happened first. **As Morrison writes,** "For years each put up with the spite in his own way, but by 1873 Sethe and her daughter Denver were its only victims."

3. **Use a comma to set off signal phrases.**
As Morrison **observes,** "The women in the house knew it and so did the children."

4. **Do not use a comma to set off signal phrases that end with the word *that*.**
Morrison writes that~~,~~ "Each one fled at once—the moment the house committed what was for him the one insult not to be borne or witnessed a second time around."

5. **The violation of rule number four enrages me, so let me repeat it: Do not use a comma to set off signal phrases that end with the word *that*.**
Do not write this:
   Morrison writes that, "The women in the house knew it and so did the children. For years each put up with the spite in his own way, but by 1873 Sethe and her daughter Denver were its only victims."

   Instead write this:
   Morrison writes that "The women in the house knew it and so did the children. For years each put up with the spite

> in his own way, but by 1873 Sethe and her daughter Denver were its only victims."

No comma. You do not need a comma. Please do not insert a comma.

6. **If the signal phrase is a complete sentence, use a colon after it instead of a comma.**
   Morrison sets the tone of the novel from its opening **words;:** "124 was spiteful. Full of a baby's venom. The women in the house knew it and so did the children. For years each put up with the spite in his own way, but by 1873 Sethe and her daughter Denver were its only victims."

7. **Place periods and commas within quotation marks.**
   Morrison writes, "Neither boy waited to see more; another kettleful of chickpeas smoking in a heap on the floor; soda crackers crumbled and strewn in a line next to the **doorsill."**

   Morrison writes, **"124 was spiteful,"** ascribing emotions to an inanimate object, in this case a house. Of course, it is not the house that is spiteful but Beloved.

8. **Place parenthetical citations after the closing quotation mark but before the period.**
   "Each one fled at once—the moment the house committed what was for him the one insult not to be borne or witnessed a second time **around" (3).**

9. **If a quotation takes up five or more lines of your essay, introduce it with a signal phrase, but instead of running the quotation into your own writing, use a block quote. (So-called because it looks like a block of words.) Start the passage by indenting two tabs. Usually, your signal phrase will be a complete sentence followed by a colon. For block quotes, you do not need quotation marks.**
   Morrison reports that the two sons cannot stand the spite and leave as soon as they **can:**

   > Neither boy waited to see more; another kettleful of chick-peas smoking in a heap on the floor; soda crackers crumbled and strewn in a line next to the doorsill. Nor did they wait

> for one of the relief periods: the weeks, months even, when nothing was disturbed. No. Each one fled at once—the moment the house committed what was for him the one insult not to be borne or witnessed a second time around.

10. In a block quote, place the parenthetical citation after the quotation. Unlike in quotations that you run into your text, the period in a block quotation goes before the citation. Nothing comes after it.

Morrison writes about the impossibility of living in such a place:

> For years each put up with the spite in his own way, but by 1873 Sethe and her daughter Denver were its only victims. The grandmother, Baby Suggs, was dead, and the sons, Howard and Buglar, had run away by the time they were thirteen years old—as soon as merely looking in a mirror shattered it (that was the signal for Buglar); as soon as two tiny hand prints appeared in the cake (that was it for **Howard). (3)**

11. Unless you really mean to, do not start a new paragraph after a block quote.

Morrison describes how the ghost infects the house:

> 124 was spiteful. Full of a baby's venom. The women in the house knew it and so did the children. For years each put up with the spite in his own way.... Each one fled at once—the moment the house committed what was for him the one insult not to be borne or witnessed a second time around. (3)

In calling the house "spiteful," Morrison ascribes emotions to an inanimate object. Of course, it is not the house that is spiteful but Beloved.

12. Use ellipses if you delete words from a quotation. Use three points if you remove text from within a sentence and four if you cut a sentence off and pick up later with a new sentence.

Morrison emphasizes how the past can haunt the present:

> 124 was spiteful. Full of a baby's venom. The women in the house knew it and so did the children. For years each put up with the spite **in his own way.... Each one fled at once—** the moment the house committed what was for him the one insult not to be borne or witnessed a second time around. (3)

13. If you quote three or fewer lines of a *poem*, run it into your sentence and separate line breaks with slash marks. The slash marks should have spaces before and after them. Instead of citing page numbers, cite line numbers.

In "Song of Myself," Whitman declares, "I celebrate myself; **/** and what I assume you shall assume **/** For every atom belonging to me, as good belongs to you" (~~page 1~~ **lines 1–3**).

Note that after you write *lines* once, you do not need to write it again. Just list the numbers.

14. If you quote four or more lines of a poem, introduce the passage with a signal phrase and use a block quote. Start the passage by indenting two tabs. As when quoting blocks of prose, you do not need quotation marks. Once again, the period comes before the citation. And here too do not start a new paragraph unless you mean to.

Whitman elaborates on his connection to the earth:

> My tongue, every atom of my blood, form'd from this
>   soil, this air,
> Born here of parents born here from parents the same,
>   and their
> parents the same,
> I, now thirty-seven years old in perfect health begin,
> Hoping to cease not till death. (6–9)

This lineage establishes his credentials as not just a poet but as an American.

Note that if a line from a poem spills over onto a second line, as the second line above does, indent the leftover part so readers understand it represents the same line and not a new one.

15. Follow the same rules for plays as you do for prose. If you quote four or fewer lines from a play, and the lines are

spoken by the same character, run the quotation into your prose and cite the act number and the scene number. Lady Macbeth frantically attempts to wash away the imagined bloodstains that symbolize her overwhelming remorse and complicity in the murders: "Out, damned spot! out, I say!—One: two: why, then, 'tis time to do't" (5.1).

16. **If you quote five or more lines of a play, introduce the passage with a signal phrase and use a block quote. Start the passage by indenting two tabs. As when quoting prose, the period—or in this case the question mark—comes before the citation. Here too do not start a new paragraph unless you mean to.** The doctor and the gentlewoman watch as Lady Macbeth frantically attempts to wash away the imagined bloodstains that symbolize her overwhelming remorse and complicity in the murders:

    > Out, damned spot! out, I say!—One: two: why,
    > then, 'tis time to do't.—Hell is murky!—Fie, my
    > lord, fie! a soldier, and afeard? What need we
    > fear who knows it, when none can call our power
    > to account?—Yet who would have thought the old
    > man to have had so much blood in him? (5.1.37–42)

    Here Lady Macbeth consoles herself by saying that even if others discover the murderous plot, they cannot do anything about it.

Afterword

We could wander so much deeper into the corn maze of numbers, titles, and quotations that we might never find our way out. If you can remember the above, however, you have a good start on following conventions.

After the Paris bartender followed me out of the bar to give me the five or six francs I had left behind—I am so old they still used francs instead of euros as the currency—I learned quickly enough to follow the convention of not tipping those who serve. Because there are more of them, and because they lack the drama of a bartender chasing you down on a city street, it will take longer to learn these conventions by heart. But write enough and you will.

Exercises

1. Fix the following sentences.
   A. A study found that approximately 30% of participants reported feeling alienated from their community, highlighting the social fragmentation present in modern society.
   B. Among the forty two artifacts uncovered at the excavation site, several showed evidence of early tool-making techniques.
   C. In a study of 75 urban neighborhoods, researchers found that social cohesion significantly reduced crime rates.
   D. In the 1920's, the Surrealist movement captivated the art world with its exploration of the unconscious mind and dream imagery.
   E. In the twentieth-century, existentialist philosophers like Jean-Paul Sartre and Simone de Beauvoir explored themes of freedom, choice, and the nature of existence.
   F. In twentieth century Latin American literature, magical realism emerged as a prominent literary style, blending fantastical elements with realistic narratives.
   G. 120 developing countries received financial aid to support infrastructure projects.
   H. Researchers found that of two hundred and fifty participants, two hundred and twenty five reported experiencing increased anxiety levels during the pandemic.
   I. Smith contends that *To the Lighthouse* "is a work of mourning, an attempt to come to terms with loss" (Nine).
   J. The deforestation rate in the Amazon rainforest has increased by 25 percent over the past decade, posing serious environmental challenges.
   K. The 18th century was a period of significant political and intellectual change, characterized by the Enlightenment and the American and French Revolutions.

2. Fix the following sentences.
   A. *A Portrait Of The Artist As A Young Man* depicts the development of a young man's artistic consciousness amid the confines of early twentieth-century Ireland.
   B. During the Civil Rights Movement, "Jet" magazine played a crucial role in shaping public opinion and disseminating news to African American communities across the United States.

C. In "Anna Karenina," Leo Tolstoy masterfully weaves together the tragic story of Anna's doomed love affair with profound insights into Russian society and the human psyche.
D. In *The Lottery*, Shirley Jackson offers a chilling story that unveils the sinister underbelly of a seemingly ordinary small town through its annual ritual.
E. "Hamlet" explores themes of revenge, madness, and the complexity of the human condition.
F. James Baldwin's essay *Down at the Cross* powerfully examines the intersections of race, religion, and identity in America.
G. *Love In The Time Of Cholera*, by Gabriel García Márquez, portrays love as enduring and transformative, set against the backdrop of a cholera epidemic in a Caribbean town.
H. The "Chicago Tribune" famously printed the premature headline "Dewey Defeats Truman" in its 1948 edition, highlighting the risks of sample bias in election forecasting.
I. *The Sound And The Fury* employs innovative narrative techniques to depict the decline of the Compson family in the post–Civil War South.
J. Thomas Paine's pamphlet "Common Sense" was instrumental in swaying public opinion in favor of American independence from British rule.
K. Through the metaphor of two diverging paths in a forest, *The Road Not Taken* explores the theme of choices and their implications.

3. The paragraph below appears on page three of *Moby Dick* by Herman Melville.

> Call me Ishmael. Some years ago—never mind how long precisely—having little or no money in my purse, and nothing particular to interest me on shore, I thought I would sail about a little and see the watery part of the world. It is a way I have of driving off the spleen and regulating the circulation. Whenever I find myself growing grim about the mouth; whenever it is a damp, drizzly November in my soul; whenever I find myself involuntarily pausing before coffin warehouses, and bringing up the rear of every funeral I meet; and especially whenever my hypos get such an upper hand of me, that it requires a strong moral principle to prevent me from deliberately stepping into

> the street, and methodically knocking people's hats off—then, I account it high time to get to sea as soon as I can. This is my substitute for pistol and ball.[2]

Fix the following sentences.

A. In the iconic opening words of *Moby Dick* the narrator declared, "Call me Ishmael."

B. The opening lines of *Moby Dick* prepare the reader for the contemplative and philosophical novel to come. "Some years ago—never mind how long precisely—having little or no money in my purse, and nothing particular to interest me on shore, I thought I would sail about a little and see the watery part of the world."

C. Ishmael grimly declares "This is my substitute for pistol and ball."

D. Ishmael justifies his going to sea by declaring that, "It is a way I have of driving off the spleen and regulating circulation."

E. Note how casually Ishmael speaks of going to sea, "Some years ago—never mind how long precisely—having little or no money in my purse, and nothing particular to interest me on shore, I thought I would sail about a little and see the watery part of the world."

F. "Some years ago—never mind how long precisely—having little or no money in my purse and nothing particular to interest me on shore", Ishmael recounts, "I thought I would sail about a little and see the watery part of the world".

G. Speaking of how going to sea fends off thoughts of suicide, Ishmael observes, "This is my substitute for ball and pistol." (1)

H. In a long passage in the opening paragraph of the novel, Ishmael describes why he has chosen to go to sea: "Call me Ishmael. Some years ago—never mind how long precisely—having little or no money in my purse, and nothing particular to interest me on shore, I thought I would sail about a little and see the watery part of the world. It is a way I have of driving off the spleen and regulating the circulation." (1)

I. In a long passage in the opening paragraph of the novel, Ishmael confesses how going to sea saves him from what today we would call depression:

> Whenever I find myself growing grim about the mouth; whenever it is a damp, drizzly November in my soul; whenever I find myself involuntarily pausing before coffin warehouses, and bringing up the rear of every funeral I meet; and especially whenever my hypos get such an upper hand of me, that it requires a strong moral principle to prevent me from deliberately stepping into the street, and methodically knocking people's hats off—then, I account it high time to get to sea as soon as I can. (1)

For Ishmael, the sea represents a reprieve from the land.

J. By way of introducing himself, Ishmael reports that "Whenever I find myself growing grim about the mouth then I account it high time to get to sea as soon as I can" (1). [Note: To see where this one goes wrong, check the full passage above.]

4. The paragraph below appears on page one of *Narrative of the Life of Frederick Douglass*. (Douglass is also the author.)

> I was born in Tuckahoe, near Hillsborough, and about twelve miles from Easton, in Talbot county, Maryland. I have no accurate knowledge of my age, never having seen any authentic record containing it. By far the larger part of the slaves know as little of their ages as horses know of theirs, and it is the wish of most masters within my knowledge to keep their slaves thus ignorant. I do not remember to have ever met a slave who could tell of his birthday. They seldom come nearer to it than planting-time, harvest-time, cherry-time, spring-time, or fall-time. A want of information concerning my own was a source of unhappiness to me even during childhood. The white children could tell their ages. I could not tell why I ought to be deprived of the same privilege. I was not allowed to make any inquiries of my master concerning it. He deemed all such inquiries on the part of a slave improper and impertinent, and evidence of a restless spirit. The nearest estimate I can give makes me now between twenty-seven and twenty-eight years of age. I come to this, from hearing my master say, some time during 1835, I was about seventeen years old.[3]

Complete the following tasks:

1. Write a sentence that quotes a passage. Use a signal phrase.
2. Write a sentence that quotes a passage. Use a signal phrase that ends with the word *that.*
3. Write a sentence that quotes a passage. Use a signal phrase that is a complete sentence.
4. Check sentences one through three. What verb tense did you use for your signal phrases? What punctuation marks did you use (or not) for your signal phrases? In the passages you quoted, where did you place the periods relative to the quotation marks?
5. If you have not already done so, for numbers one through three include parenthetical citations. Where did you place the citations relative to the quotation marks and period?
6. Write a sentence that quotes a passage of five or more lines. Use a signal phrase to introduce the passage.
7. Check sentence six. What form did your signal phrase take? What punctuation mark did it use? Did the quoted passage occur in your prose? Or did you use a block quote? Did the passage have quotation marks? Where did the parenthetical citation go? Where did the closing period go? When you returned to your own writing, did you start a new paragraph?
8. Write a sentence that removes words from the middle of a quotation. How do you convey to readers that you have done so?

CHAPTER 10

Inclusion

In the wake of the Civil Rights movement and the assassination of Martin Luther King in 1968, colleges and universities sought to increase the number of minority students and faculty on their campuses. Over the next fifty years, these efforts gradually changed how universities decided which students to admit, which faculty to hire, and how to welcome marginalized groups to campus. After the murder of George Floyd in 2020, colleges and universities recommitted themselves to these goals. The programs and offices associated with them went by many names, but they eventually became known, to themselves and to the public, as DEI: Diversity, Equity, and Inclusion.

In recent years, some states, notably Texas and Florida, have banned public universities from spending state money on DEI initiatives, a decision that predictably gutted these programs. As I write, the Trump administration has declared total war on anything remotely associated with diversity, equity, or inclusion. I regret these developments, because I think universities and colleges have work left to do to become more just places. That said, and regardless of what, if anything, survives this institutional purge, a respect for diversity, equity, and inclusion necessarily affects how we write and how we think about writing.

This chapter takes up two issues that follow from concerns about diversity, equity, and inclusion. The first addresses sexist language and pronouns. The second treats what its proponents call linguistic justice. To my mind, the advice about avoiding sexist language and using inclusive pronouns is more or less settled. The same cannot be said for the issue of linguistic justice, which remains controversial and, perhaps, irresolvable. I raise it not because I have the answer, but because students should know the question.

Pronouns

Of the three values on offer in the formula diversity, equity, and inclusion, the last may matter the most for writing. You do not know who will read your writing. Therefore, you want to offend as few readers as possible. Or, to state the matter positively, you want to welcome—to include—as many readers as possible.

What does it mean to include as many readers as possible? To start, it means not relying on stereotypes and, as part of that commitment, not using sexist language. For example, it may have once made sense to speak of *congressmen*, back when only men served in Congress, but continuing to refer to *congressmen* ignores the women who represent their states and districts in Congress. To avoid alienating readers, a writer should use a gender-neutral word like *representative*, *legislator*, or *member of Congress*. The same goes for words like *fireman*, *freshman*, and *mankind*. Far better to say *firefighter*, *first-year student*, or *people*. To be sure, some readers will accuse a writer who uses gender-neutral terms of bowing to political correctness, but I doubt many readers will notice if a writer substitutes *first-year student* for *freshman*. Many readers, however, will notice if a writer persists in using *freshman*.

Sexist language can arise not just in nouns but in pronouns. For example, what is wrong with the following sentence:

> In Pennsylvania, for instance, an elementary school teacher must renew her certification every five years.

A stereotype projects certain fixed traits onto a group of people. By referring to "her" certification, the sentence above circulates the stereotype that all elementary school teachers are women because, perhaps, only women are good with children. Neither of these assertions is true.

Below I demonstrate how to fix sentences like this one, but for now notice that we have wandered into the thicket of appropriate pronouns. In chapter four, you learned that a pronoun is a word that stands in for a noun (or a noun phrase). The problem is that English has no gender-neutral third person singular pronoun. It has *he*, and it has *she*, but that is it. Yet often, as in the sentence about the elementary school teacher, a writer very much needs a gender-neutral third person pronoun.

For most of the history of the English language, indeed until quite recently, writers let *he* stand in for *he or she*. In other words, *he*—often referred to as the generic *he*—functioned as the standard gender-neutral third person pronoun even though it was not, well, gender neutral. As a result, you would often find sentences like this one:

> If a student wants to succeed in his studies, he must be diligent and dedicated.

Just as not all elementary school teachers are women, not all students are men. For centuries, however, grammarians held that the *he* in this sentence did not refer to men alone but to men and women. Hence the so-called generic *he*. Everyone understood, or was supposed to understand, that *he* stood in for the clumsy phrase *he or she*.

Yet even proponents of the generic *he* admitted that it occasionally led to absurd sentences like the following one:

> There must be opportunity for the individual boy or girl to go as far as his keenness and ability will take him.

That sentence comes from the venerable H. W. Fowler, whom we met in chapter five. Fowler defended the generic *he* but also recognized, as in the sentence above, that it had its faults. For Fowler, however, the generic *he* had fewer faults than any other solution.[1]

Later critics, however, weighed the matter differently. Perhaps no one captured the absurdities of the generic *he* better than the science fiction writer Ursula K. Le Guin, who offered this example:

> If a person needs an abortion, he should be required to tell his parents.[2]

For Le Guin and other writers, the generic *he* did not just lead to ridiculous sentences like this one. Whether by design or not, these critics asserted, the generic *he* excludes women. Beginning in the 1970s, more and more people, both women and men, agreed with that argument.

So, what to use instead? Grammarians and non-grammarians offered a number of options. Some called for a return to *he or she*. Others wanted to counterbalance centuries of the generic *he* by using the generic *she*. Yet that solution created its own problem. The generic *she* could reproduce sexist sentences like the one quoted above: "In Pennsylvania, for example, an elementary school teacher must renew her certification every five years." Some grammarians wanted to avoid the issue altogether. They proposed rewriting sentences, usually by turning the singular noun into a plural one and, thus, recasting the troublesome singular pronoun as a plural one. That sounds more complicated than it is. The previous sentence about a student would simply look like this:

> If ~~a student wants~~ **students want** to succeed in ~~his~~ **their** studies, ~~he~~ **they** must be diligent and dedicated.

Problem solved.

Yet many people argued that options like *he or she*, the generic *she*, or even turning singular nouns into plural ones were solutions in search of a problem. In reality, there was no problem. English already had a perfectly good word for the gender-neutral third person singular pronoun. It was *they*. Sticklers might complain about this usage. For them, *they* was a plural pronoun. It thus made no sense to write a sentence like this one:

> An individual is free only when they can choose and act according to their own volitions and convictions.

"An individual" is singular. "They" is plural. As a rule, singular nouns demand singular pronouns. Yet even the sticklers had to admit that in addition to everyday speakers, a roster of revered writers (William Shakespeare, Jane Austen, Virginia Woolf) had used the singular *they*.

What is more, English already had a precedent for a pronoun that did double-duty as both singular and plural: *you*. Here is a sentence spoken to a single first-year student:

> If you want to succeed in life, you must be willing to take risks.

And here is a sentence spoken to an assembly of first-year students:

> If you want to succeed in life, you must be willing to take risks.

A few grammarians still flinch when they see the singular *they*, but fewer and fewer. Speakers have always used the word. So too writers. And as time passes, more and more writers will, even in formal writing.

The singular *they* has another advantage. At a time when many people reject gender binaries, the singular *they* recognizes that not everyone fits neatly into either-or pronouns like *he* or *she*, *him* or *her*, and *his* or *hers*. For example, here is a sentence about the literary critic Judith Butler, who identifies as they:

> Judith Butler is a prominent philosopher and gender theorist known for their work on gender performativity. They argue that gender is not an inherent quality, but rather a social construct that is performed and repeated through actions and behaviors.

I admit that I sometimes stumble over the pronoun *they* when it begins a sentence and refers to a singular person, as the second of these sentences does. But I think that just means I am old. I suspect younger generations will barely notice it.

In any case, all signs point to the pronouns *they*, *them*, and *their*, which is good, not just for the English language but for writers who want to include as many readers—men, women, and nonbinary—as possible.

Linguistic Justice

Thanks to the singular *they*, writers discovered (or rediscovered) an elegant solution to pronoun inclusion. The issue of linguistic justice has not had a similar breakthrough. It remains, and likely will remain, a dilemma.

What is linguistic justice? It starts from the premise that all dialects of English are created equal. (A dialect is a version of a language associated with a region or social group.) If the purpose of language is to communicate, then any language—or dialect of that language—that does so counts as a language. English has many dialects, but those who argue for linguistic justice focus on what they call Black English and White Mainstream English. These dialects have different features, but those features do not make one dialect superior to the other. For example, Black English has what linguists call the habitual *be*. "She be going to class every morning." Nothing makes that usage inherently better or worse than the equivalent sentence in White Mainstream English, that is, "She goes to class every morning."

Of course, not all Black people use Black English, but enough do that it has become associated with a single race. Of the two dialects, however, only one (Black English) is labeled a dialect. The other (White Mainstream English) is treated not as a dialect but as the standard from which other dialects depart. In reality, however, White Mainstream English is also a dialect. Although it purports to be a neutral standard, it is drawn, as the linguist Rosina Lippi-Green argues, "primarily from the spoken language of the upper middle class."[3] White Mainstream English also functions as the standard written language, which, again, other dialects supposedly fail to live up to.

Here is where the trouble starts. Favoring one dialect (White Mainstream English) over another (Black English) is a form of linguistic discrimination. Just as one race is declared better than another, one dialect is declared better than another. Nor does the discrimination stop with language. Linguistic discrimination causes and is an effect of discrimination writ large. "The marginalization, colonization, exploitation, policing, and stereotypes associated with Black English," April Baker-Bell writes, "is linked to a system of white supremacy."[4] In other words, the symbolic violence done to Black English may enable real violence against Black people, violence that, in the age of Black Lives Matter, has become all too common.

Less dramatically, but no less crucially, in being taught to reject Black English, Black students are taught to reject themselves. After all, if their language is held in such low regard, it follows that the speakers of that language are or should be held in equally low regard, even by the speakers themselves. As Baker-Bell writes, when White Mainstream English is the standard, Black students learn "to correlate blackness with wrongness and whiteness with rightness."[5] Put differently, by internalizing the contempt for their language, Black students may learn to feel an equal contempt for themselves and their race.

In the past, Black students navigated these waters by practicing code-switching. With their friends and families, Black students would speak Black English. In classrooms and workplaces, they would switch to speaking—and writing—White Mainstream English. Yet asking Black students to code-switch still devalues Black English. That dialect may have a life outside of classrooms, the thinking goes, but it does not belong in classrooms. It is a second-class language. Moreover, asking Black students to speak a language that is not their own puts them at a disadvantage to students who grew up hearing, speaking, and writing White Mainstream English. (Those for whom English is a second language face a similar problem.) If white students use the language that comes naturally to them, why should Black students not enjoy the same privilege?

What should be done about this string of injustices? A lot of things, but everything starts with dismantling the assumption that Black English is wrong and White Mainstream English is right. If so, then that approach would challenge the very idea of a book like this one. It teaches students how to write better White Mainstream English. It does not, except for this chapter, challenge the supremacy of the dialect that masquerades as a standard. In teaching students how to write White Mainstream English better, rather than, say, making the case for Black English, this book makes it all the harder to end linguistic discrimination and achieve linguistic justice.

In sum, if pronouns aspire to include as many readers as possible, linguistic justice aspires to include as many writers and as many types of written English as possible.

I have enormous sympathy for this argument. I also have some misgivings. Proponents of linguistic justice have much to say about what should and should not happen in writing classrooms, but few say much about what should happen in other classrooms or in workplaces. All students, but especially Black students, will need to learn how to write White Mainstream English lest they lose out, in their classes and careers, to other writers who have learned how to do so.

This impasse makes the cliché *damned if you do, damned if you don't* especially relevant. If teachers teach students how to write White Mainstream English better, they perpetuate linguistic discrimination. Yet if teachers focus on linguistic discrimination, they risk disappointing students, including Black ones, who want to earn a degree and find the job college prepared them to find. In many if not most of those jobs, students will need to have if not perfected then at least practiced White Mainstream English. As I say, damned if you do, damned if you don't.

In a perfect world, Black English and White Mainstream English would have the same status. Alas, that perfect world does not exist and may never exist. What to do in the meantime? My imperfect solution is to teach students how to write well *and* to teach them that learning how to write well unfolds against a backdrop of linguistic discrimination and injustice. That is the definition of a half-measure, maybe even a quarter-measure, but I see no alternative.

I would add one more thing. As I write in the introduction to this book, I hope that in taking care of style—concision, sentence fragments, avoiding the passive voice—writers can cultivate their own style, their own voice. That formula may apply to Black students most of all, who could bring their own dialect—their own voice—to their writing. In other words, Black writers would not be compelled to code-switch but invited to do what Vershawn Ashanti Young and others call code-mesh.[6] If so, Black writers can take advantage of Black English, using it to distinguish their prose from the lifeless prose generated by artificial intelligence, which is trained almost exclusively on White Mainstream English.[7] Of course, Black students incorporating their dialect into their prose would not fulfill all the hopes for a more inclusive form of writing. But it would make a start.

CHAPTER 11

Putting It All Together: Quizzes

With the help of ChatGPT, I have assembled the passages below to include most of the style issues covered in the chapters of this book: (1) wordy phrases; (2) redundant phrases; (3) paired words; (4) the passive voice; (5) misplaced or dangling modifiers; (6) faulty parallelism; (7) vague pronouns; (8) clichés; (9) sentence fragments; (10) run-on sentences; (11) the serial comma—or lack thereof; (12) pretentious diction; and (13) conventions for numbers, titles, and quotations. Find the errors in each passage and fix them. I have helped you with the first passage by boldfacing where an error occurs. For the last two paragraphs, you are on your own. For all three, keep track of which of the errors listed above you have spotted. If you have not found one, you can hunt specifically for it. With one or two exceptions, each sentence has only one error.

1. In **"Macbeth,"** guilt pervades the narrative and drives the characters to commit heinous acts. Guilt in the play manifests in three main ways: hallucinations and visions, physical manifestations like sleepwalking, and **how the mental states of its characters slowly deteriorate.** Lady Macbeth descends into madness **due to the fact that** she cannot escape the overwhelming guilt stemming from Duncan's murder. **Tortured by guilt, the sleepwalking scene** vividly portrays her inner turmoil. Her guilt drives her to madness, proving that **"what goes around comes around." Because she cannot escape her guilt.**

   Macbeth's guilt is exacerbated by his **past history** of ambition, **ruthlessness and relentless** pursuit of power. The murder of King Duncan **is regretted by Macbeth**. Harassed by his conscience, Macbeth confesses **that,** "full of scorpions is my **mind. (2.2)"**

Both Macbeth and Lady Macbeth are consumed by **remorse and regret** for their treacherous deed. **This** weighs heavily on their minds and souls, driving them to madness and despair**,** **it** is a stark reminder of the consequences unchecked ambition and moral transgression can have. The characters are tormented by **an ineffable sense of peccability,** as they **encounter the irrevocable moral transgressions** that **besiege** their every waking moment.

2. Reading through social media posts, time flies by. Social media has transformed how people consume news, connect with others, and accessing entertainment. Profoundly impacting society in both positive and negative ways.

   Social media platforms offer users a variety of features, including messaging, photo sharing and live streaming. It allows people to connect and communicate with others, even when they are not in close proximity. Social media offers an endless and infinite array of content. Its platforms have catalyzed a paradigm shift in interpersonal communication, fostering unprecedented levels of interconnectivity and information dissemination.

   Social media undoubtedly creates these opportunities, however, excessive use can cause feelings of isolation and anxiety, especially among young women. Social media amplifies their insecurities, leading to increased rates of anxiety and depression. On social media, a well-crafted image can often convey a message more effectively than a lengthy post, truly exemplifying the adage a picture is worth a thousand words. This can lead to a distorted perception of reality, contributing to poor self-esteem and body image issues. As Donna Jackson Nakazawa explains in *Girls On The Brink* "When we look at the mental health of American girls, one thing becomes clear: We as a society are failing pretty miserably (xi)."

   More regulation of social media is deemed necessary by many. In the event that social media usage continues to rise unchecked, its effect on mental health could become increasingly concerning.

3. Redlining was a discriminatory practice used by banks, companies and other financial institutions to deny or limit mortgage loans or insurance to certain neighborhoods based on their racial

or ethnic composition. The term originated from the practice of lenders drawing red lines on maps to delineate areas where they would not invest, these areas were often characterized by high concentrations of minority residents, particularly African Americans and Latinos. In the 1930's, the Home Owners' Loan Corporation (HOLC) redlined around 85 neighborhoods in Chicago.

Redlining practices were unfair and unjust, as they systematically favored certain racial groups while discriminating against others. Redlining led to inequalities across the board: in restricted access to housing; in limited educational opportunities; and it diminished economic prospects for many communities. The end result was the creation of segregated neighborhoods, with lasting effects on community development and wealth accumulation.

Even though redlining led to disparities in wealth, housing, and opportunity. Redlining was criticized by activists for perpetuating systemic discrimination in housing markets. Determined to address the issue, the practice was swiftly condemned by the committee devoted to drawing up the Fair Housing Act of 1968.

In spite of the fact that redlining was officially banned in the 1960s, its legacy continues to affect communities of color in any number of ways. This is evident in the unequal distribution of resources, which perpetuated a cycle of disadvantage for marginalized communities. Despite efforts to ameliorate its impacts, redlining entrenched systemic inequities and exacerbated socioeconomic disparities for generations. Banks and lending institutions promised equal opportunity, but actions speak louder than words.

Answers to Exercises

Some exercises have more than one answer or approach. I include the ones that seemed likeliest to me.

Chapter 1

1. Substitute one word for the whole phrase.
   A. An artist who ~~has the opportunity to~~ **can** study under a master painter gains not only technical skills but also a deep understanding of the artistic traditions and techniques passed down through generations.
   B. ~~In the near future, further~~ Further research into the artist's lesser-known sketches may **soon** provide deeper insights into their evolving creative process.
   C. ~~Considering the fact that~~ **Since [or Because]** the Renaissance period marked a significant revival of interest in classical art and learning, it is not surprising that many artists of the time sought to emulate the styles and techniques of ancient Greek and Roman art.
   D. ~~It is crucial that art~~ **Art** historians **must** carefully examine the brushstrokes and color palette of the painting to determine the artist's stylistic influences and the historical context in which it was created.
   E. ~~It is possible that the~~ **The** shift in the artist's color palette during this period ~~reflects~~ **might reflect** a deeper emotional or philosophical evolution in his work.

F. ~~In light of the fact that~~ **Since [or Because]** the artist was deeply influenced by the Romantic movement, his paintings often depict dramatic landscapes with a sense of sublime beauty and awe-inspiring nature.
G. ~~In reference to~~ **Concerning** the artist's use of light and shadow, scholars have noted a similarity between his techniques and those employed by Baroque painters to create a sense of depth and drama in their compositions.
H. ~~In spite of the fact that~~ **Although** the artist faced criticism for his unconventional techniques, his paintings are now celebrated for their innovative approach to color and form.
I. ~~In the event that~~ **If** new evidence comes to light regarding the provenance of the painting, art historians may need to reassess its attribution to determine its true origins.
J. ~~A number of~~ **Some** Renaissance artists, such as Leonardo da Vinci and Michelangelo, revolutionized the art world with their innovative techniques and profound artistic vision.

2. Take or adapt one word from the definition to create your own redundant phrase.
   A. **Quickly** accelerate
   B. **Exciting** adventure
   C. **Gratefully** appreciate
   D. **Surrounding** environment
   E. **Interestingly** fascinating
   F. **Brightly** illuminate
   G. **Unbelievably** inconceivable
   H. **Impossibly** incredible
   I. **Notably** memorable
   J. **Possible** opportunities

3. Cut the extra word or words.
   A. After extensive debate, the committee reached a ~~definite~~ decision regarding the allocation of funds for the public health initiative.
   B. During ~~the course of~~ the election campaign, the candidate's stance on key issues evolved in response to changing public opinion and political dynamics.
   C. In his proposal, the candidate spells out ~~in detail~~ his plan for economic reform, outlining specific policy measures and their expected outcomes.

D. In political science, understanding the ~~basic~~ fundamentals of democratic governance is essential for analyzing the effectiveness of different political systems in promoting citizen participation and accountability.
E. The ~~close~~ proximity of the two countries has led to frequent border disputes, highlighting the importance of diplomacy and conflict resolution in maintaining regional stability.
F. The decision to postpone the vote on the bill ~~until later~~ reflects the government's recognition of the need for further consultation and deliberation with stakeholders.
G. An analysis of the nation's ~~past~~ history reveals recurring patterns of political instability following economic crises.
H. The formation of policy often requires a consensus ~~of opinion~~ among political leaders, reflecting the complex interplay of competing interests and ideologies within a society.
I. The government's decision to revert ~~back~~ to its previous foreign policy stance surprised many observers, signaling a shift in diplomatic strategy.
J. The negotiation process for the trade agreement was arduous, but the document is now ~~completely~~ finished and ready for ratification by the participating countries.

Chapter 2

1. Which of these sentences is in the active voice and which in the passive voice?
   A. Archaeologists unearthed the ancient city's ruins during their latest excavation. **[Active]**
   B. The book was written by Mark Twain. [**Passive**]
   C. The anthropologist analyzed artifacts excavated from the ancient burial site to understand burial practices and cultural beliefs. [**Active**]
   D. The concept of the "self" has been debated by philosophers for centuries. [**Passive**]
   E. The poet Homer crafted the epic poems the *Iliad* and the *Odyssey* during the eighth century BCE. [**Active**]
   F. The effects of the therapy were studied extensively over a period of several years. [**Passive**]
   G. The novel was translated into over fifty languages, highlighting its global appeal. [**Passive**]

H. The researchers administered surveys to a random sample of households to assess their attitudes toward government policies. **[Active]**
I. The play was directed by a renowned theater director known for his innovative approach to staging. **[Passive]**
J. Scholars have debated the interpretation of this religious text for centuries. **[Active]**

2. Turn these active-voice sentences into passive-voice ones.
   A. Plymouth Colony **was founded by** the Pilgrims in 1620.
   B. The Continental Army during the American Revolutionary War **was led by** George Washington.
   C. The Articles of Confederation **were drafted by** the Founding Fathers in 1777.
   D. The Western territories of the United States **were explored by** Lewis and Clark from 1804 to 1806.
   E. The famous debates with Stephen A. Douglas **were conducted by** Abraham Lincoln during the Illinois Senate race of 1858.
   F. The office of President of the United States **was held by** Theodore Roosevelt from 1901 to 1909.
   G. The New Deal programs **were implemented by** Franklin D. Roosevelt during the Great Depression in the 1930s.
   H. The Montgomery Bus Boycott **was started** in 1955 when Rosa Parks refused to give up her seat to a white man.
   I. The iconic "I Have a Dream" speech **was delivered by** Martin Luther King Jr. during the March on Washington for Jobs and Freedom in 1963.
   J. During the Apollo 11 mission in 1969, the moon **was walked on** by Neil Armstrong and Buzz Aldrin.

3. Turn these passive-voice sentences into active-voice ones.
   A. Thomas Jefferson **wrote** the Declaration of Independence.
   B. President Abraham Lincoln **issued** the Emancipation Proclamation during the Civil War.
   C. Delegates at the Constitutional Convention in 1787 **signed** the United States Constitution.
   D. President Thomas Jefferson **negotiated** the Louisiana Purchase in 1803, doubling the size of the United States.
   E. President Abraham Lincoln **delivered** the Gettysburg Address during the American Civil War.

F. President Lyndon B. Johnson **signed** into law the Civil Rights Act of 1964, prohibiting discrimination based on race, color, religion, sex, or national origin.
G. American scientists **led** the Manhattan Project during World War II, resulting in the development of the atomic bomb.
H. The Supreme Court **decided** the landmark *Brown v. Board of Education* case in 1954, overturning segregation in public schools.
I. The United States **implemented** the Marshall Plan to aid European countries in rebuilding after World War II.
J. Courageous activists fighting for equal voting rights **led** the women's suffrage movement in the nineteenth century.

4. Write a paragraph that features the framers as the subject:

The framers of the Constitution, including notable figures like James Madison, Alexander Hamilton, and Benjamin Franklin, ~~were~~ **convened** in Philadelphia during the Constitutional Convention of 1787. Their primary goal was to address the weaknesses of the Articles of Confederation and to create a more effective system of governance. ~~A~~ **The framers established** a system of checks and balances ~~was established by the framers~~ to balance power between the federal government and the states. Through compromise and debate, **the framers crafted** a document ~~was crafted by the framers~~ that established principles of democracy, including the protection of individual rights and freedoms. Despite differing viewpoints and backgrounds, **the framers demonstrated** remarkable unity and commitment to creating an enduring government ~~were demonstrated by the framers~~.

5. Write a paragraph that features the Constitution (or its characteristics) as the subject:

The Constitution of the United States, ratified in 1788, is regarded as the supreme law of the land, having been established to provide a framework for the nation's government. A system of checks and balances was established by the framers to balance power between the federal government and the states. Through compromise and debate, a document was crafted by the framers that established principles of democracy, including the protection of individual rights and freedoms. Provisions for amendments were included in the Constitution, indicating the framers' foresight in allowing for the document's adaptation to changing times and circumstances. The enduring legacy of the Constitution is found in its ability to serve as a foundation for democracy, providing a framework for governance that has guided the United States for over two centuries.

Chapter 3

3. Fix the following five sentences by resurrecting a verb from a noun.
    A. The movie *To Kill a Mockingbird* ~~is an adaptation of~~ **adapts** Harper Lee's novel of the same name, translating its themes and characters to the screen.
    B. In many religions, the microcosm of the individual ~~is a mirror of~~ **mirrors** the macrocosm of the universe.
    C. The concept of supply and demand ~~is a description of~~ **describes** the relationship between the availability of a good or service (supply) and the desire of consumers to purchase it (demand).
    D. One of the key sentences of the Second Amendment ~~is its reference~~ **refers** to a "well regulated Militia."
    E. The development of a child's personality ~~is dependent upon~~ **depends upon** genetic predispositions and environmental influences.

4. These five sentences need a new subject as well as a new verb before you can fix them.
    A. ~~There is a long-standing debate in philosophy about~~ **Philosophers have debated** the nature of reality and whether it is ultimately material or immaterial.
    B. ~~It is evident that social inequality~~ **Scholars believe social inequality pervades** contemporary society, impacting access to resources and opportunities based on factors such as race, class, and gender.
    C. ~~There are differing perspectives within anthropology~~ **Anthropologists differ** on the impact of globalization on traditional cultural practices.

D. ~~It is widely argued that~~ **Feminists argue that** gender is a complex and multifaceted social construct, shaped by a variety of factors including culture, biology, and individual identity.

E. ~~Studying these artists is a way to~~ **By studying these artists, we can** gain a deeper understanding of their creative process, influences, and the historical context in which they worked.

Chapter 4

2. Fix these misplaced and dangling modifiers.
   A. Trying to paper over their differences, **Congress** passed the Fugitive Slave Act in 1850.
   B. Surviving centuries, **the artifacts** are carefully preserved by the museum.
   C. Having struggled with mental illness, **Virginia Woolf** provided a unique perspective on the human psyche in her novel *Mrs. Dalloway*.
   D. Written into law in 1850, the Fugitive Slave Act angered many Northerners.
   E. Maneuvering for political advantage, **state representatives** redrew the district boundaries to influence election outcomes.

4. Fix these examples of non-parallel sentences.
   A. Judaism is characterized by its monotheistic belief in one God, the Torah, and ~~observing~~ traditional Jewish laws and customs.
   B. Rhyme is a poetic device that enhances musicality, ~~creating~~ **creates** rhythm, and **drives** the memorability of verse.
   C. In the realm of penal systems, it is often more challenging to rehabilitate offenders than ~~incarcerating~~ **to incarcerate** them.
   D. Gospel music played a pivotal role in the civil rights movement by providing spiritual strength, ~~it spread~~ **spreading** messages of hope and resilience, and ~~its mobilization of~~ **mobilizing** communities for social change.
   E. Critics of fracking argue that it can lead to groundwater contamination, ~~the air being polluted~~ **air pollution**, and minor earthquakes ~~that can nevertheless be measured on the Richter scale~~.

5. Write two transitions for the start of the second paragraph that ties it to the previous paragraph.
   A. **Loneliness has physical as well as mental effects.** Studies have found...
   B. **In addition,** studies have found...

7. Fix these vague pronouns (and the accompanying verb) by filling in the blanks.
   A. Propaganda is a form of communication that is used to influence the attitudes, beliefs, and behaviors of a group of people. This **technique** is often used in politics, advertising, and public relations to shape public opinion and promote a particular agenda.
   B. Religion plays a crucial role in many communities, providing a sense of identity, belonging, and moral guidance to its members. This **role** often serves as a foundation for community values and traditions, shaping social interactions and collective rituals.
   C. Economic inequality refers to the unequal distribution of income and wealth among individuals or groups within a society. This **inequality** often leads to social and economic challenges, such as limited access to education, healthcare, and opportunities for upward mobility.
   D. The use of social media platforms by influencers and celebrities can shape perceptions and influence trends among their followers. These **effects** often lead to depression.
   E. The colonization of indigenous lands by European powers had profound and lasting effects on native populations and their way of life. This **history of conquest** imposed new laws and practices on what had been stable cultures.

Chapter 5

1. Underline the images and clichés that form the mixed metaphors.
   A. The foundation of his argument begins to unravel as it drowns in a sea of contradictory evidence.
   B. The market was a powder keg waiting to explode, but policymakers managed to weather the storm by injecting liquidity into the system.

C. The movement for gender equality gained traction, breaking the glass ceiling while planting seeds of change across society.
D. The speaker's message was a lightning rod that sparked a wave of dialogue, but it quickly ran out of steam as the audience lost interest.
E. In the work of the playwright Tom Stoppard, the dialogue dances like a flame, illuminating the complexities of human nature while anchoring the narrative in a whirlwind of philosophical inquiry.

2. Underline the clichés in these paragraphs. (There may be more than one.) Try to fix the sentences by using each of the first three strategies for rooting out clichés: cut it, translate it, or invent something better.
   A. The economic recession hit the country hard, but there is light at the end of the tunnel as recovery efforts gain momentum.
   B. The phrase "divide and conquer" describes a key strategy employed by colonial powers to exert control over indigenous populations.
   C. The state faced many challenges in implementing the new policy, but every cloud has a silver lining, and there is hope that the policy will be better off because of these initial difficulties.

3. Underline the clichés you see and then apply whichever of the four strategies (cut, translate, invent, or sacrifice one for another) you think will fix the sentence and paragraph best.

   Take the example of a business owner who is just starting out. They may have a vision for their company and a plan to make it successful, but they will face roadblocks along the way. Perhaps their initial marketing efforts fail to pay off, or they struggle to find the right man for the right job who will help grow their business.

   In these situations, it can be easy to become discouraged and retreat with your tail tucked between your legs. However, those who are able to stay the course are much more likely to achieve success. By learning from their mistakes and remembering that Rome wasn't built in a day, they can eventually build a thriving business that fulfills their wildest dreams.

Chapter 6

2. Diagnose what each lacks (subject, verb, complete thought, or all three), and then add what it needs to make it a bona fide sentence.
   A. In *The Fire Next Time*, James Baldwin vividly illustrating the urgency of racial equality. **[Verb]**
   B. In *The Fire Next Time*, vividly illustrates the urgency of racial equality. **[Subject]**
   C. Although in *The Fire Next Time* James Baldwin vividly illustrates the urgency of racial equality. **[Complete thought]**
   D. In *The Fire Next Time*, vividly illustrating the urgency of racial equality. **[All three]**
   E. Free will, a concept central to philosophy and theology, raising fundamental questions about human agency and the nature of existence. **[Verb]**
   F. A concept central to philosophy and theology, raises fundamental questions about human agency and the nature of existence. **[Subject]**
   G. A concept central to philosophy and theology, raising fundamental questions about human agency and the nature of existence. **[All three]**
   H. Raising fundamental questions about human agency and the nature of existence. **[All three]**
   I. The discriminatory practice that systematically denied loans and services to people in certain neighborhoods based on race, redlining continuing to have lasting effects on housing patterns and wealth disparities in the United States. **[Verb]**
   J. The discriminatory practice that systematically denied loans and services to people in certain neighborhoods based on race, continues to have lasting effects on housing patterns and wealth disparities in the United States. **[Subject]**
   K. The discriminatory practice that systematically denied loans and services to people in certain neighborhoods based on race, continuing to have lasting effects on housing patterns and wealth disparities in the United States. **[All three]**
   L. While redlining, the discriminatory practice that systematically denied loans and services to people in certain neighborhoods based on race, continues to have lasting effects on housing patterns and wealth disparities in the United States. **[Complete Thought]**

3. Here are three run-on sentences about cave painting. Fix them by using each of the strategies you learned in this chapter.
   A. Cave painting dates back tens of thousands of **years, and it** is one of the earliest forms of human artistic expression.

      Cave painting dates back tens of thousands of **years; it** is one of the earliest forms of human artistic expression.

      Cave painting dates back tens of thousands of **years. It** is one of the earliest forms of human artistic expression.

      Since cave painting dates back tens of thousands of **years, it** is one of the earliest forms of human artistic expression.
   B. These paintings were created with supposedly crude techniques like finger painting, blowing pigment through tubes, and using brushes made from animal hair, **yet** they depict a wide range of subjects such as animals, human figures, abstract symbols, and scenes of daily life.

      These paintings were created with supposedly crude techniques like finger painting, blowing pigment through tubes, and using brushes made from animal hair; **nevertheless,** they depict a wide range of subjects such as animals, human figures, abstract symbols, and scenes of daily life.

      These paintings were created with supposedly crude techniques like finger painting, blowing pigment through tubes, and using brushes made from animal **hair. Nevertheless, they** depict a wide range of subjects such as animals, human figures, abstract symbols, and scenes of daily life.

      Although these paintings were created with supposedly crude techniques like finger painting, blowing pigment through tubes, and using brushes made from animal **hair, they** depict a wide range of subjects such as animals, human figures, abstract symbols, and scenes of daily life.
   C. Archaeologists admire cave paintings for their aesthetic value, **for** they offer valuable insights into the beliefs, practices, and environments of early humans.

      Archeologists admire cave paintings for their aesthetic **value; they** offer valuable insights into the beliefs, practices, and environments of early humans.

      Archeologists admire cave paintings for their aesthetic **value. They** offer valuable insights into the beliefs, practices, and environments of early humans.

Archeologists admire cave paintings for their aesthetic value **because** they offer valuable insights into the beliefs, practices, and environments of early humans.

4. Do you need a comma in any of the following sentences? Add one, take one out, or do nothing.
   A. Disparities in access to quality education contribute to persistent gaps in academic achievement~~,~~ and opportunities for students from marginalized communities. **[Remove comma.]**
   B. Deregulation reduced government intervention in the airline industry and led to increased competition, lower prices for consumers**,** and greater innovation. **[Add comma.]**
   C. Magical thinking may seem irrational**,** but it often serves as a coping mechanism or a way to find meaning in the world. **[Add comma.]**
   D. In 1848, Phineas Gage survived an explosion that sent an iron rod through his skull**,** but the accident dramatically changed his personality. **[Add comma.]**
   E. Terrorism remains a global threat~~,~~ and instills fear across nations. **[Remove comma.]**

5. Find the errors and revise the paragraph.

Abolitionism, a transformative social and political movement, emerged in the eighteenth century with the goal of eradicating the institution of slavery. Rooted in the principles of human rights and equality, ~~arguing~~ **abolitionists argued** vehemently against the dehumanizing practice of slavery~~,~~ and ~~advocating~~ **advocated** for the immediate emancipation of enslaved individuals. Central to the abolitionist movement was the belief that slavery was morally wrong~~,~~ and fundamentally incompatible with the values of a just and humane society.

Abolitionists employed a variety of tactics to advance their cause, including public lectures, composing anti-slavery literature, organizing boycotts**,** and participating in direct action such as the Underground Railroad, a network of secret routes and safe houses that helped enslaved individuals escape to freedom. Key figures in the abolitionist movement, such as Frederick Douglass, Harriet Tubman, and William Lloyd Garrison, played instrumental roles in raising awareness about the brutal realities of slavery~~,~~**.** ~~they~~ **They** galvanized public support for its abolition.

Abolitionists faced staunch opposition from pro-slavery interests, particularly in the Southern United States where the economy depended heavily on slave labor~~,~~**;** however, they remained steadfast in their commitment to their cause. ~~Although~~ **Their** efforts bore fruit with the abolition of slavery in many countries, including the United States with the ratification of the 13th Amendment in 1865. The abolitionist movement stands as a testament to the power of activism, and it illustrates the power of activism to effect lasting change.

Chapter 8

1. Look up the etymology of the words below. Which come from Anglo-Saxon? Which from Latin?
   A. Bold [**Anglo-Saxon**]
   B. Cognition [**Latin**]
   C. Earth [**Anglo-Saxon**]
   D. Evil [**Anglo-Saxon**]
   E. House [**Anglo-Saxon**]
   F. Jurisdiction [**Latin**]
   G. Nominate [**Latin**]
   H. Old [**Anglo-Saxon**]
   I. Rejuvenate [**Latin**]
   J. Spectacle [**Latin**]
   K. Wonder [**Anglo-Saxon**]
   L. Work [**Anglo-Saxon**]

2. Take the Latin words from Exercise One and break them into their component parts. What other English words do their parts form?
   B. Cognition = **Incognito**
   F. Jurisdiction = **Jury**
   G. Nominate = **Nominal**
   I. Rejuvenate = **Juvenile**
   J. Spectacle = **Inspect**

3. Find synonyms for these possibly pretentious words.
   A. Cacophonous = **Harsh**
   B. Confabulate = **Make up**
   C. Concupiscence = **Lust**

D. Ebullient = **Exuberant**
E. Ineffable = **Indescribable**
F. Genuflect = **Humble**
G. Lugubrious = **Mournful**
H. Mellifluous = **Sweet (of a voice or sound)**
I. Noetic = **Mystical**
J. Obfuscate = **Hide**
K. Perambulate = **Walk**
L. Perspicacious = **Insightful**
M. Prolixity = **Wordy**
N. Quixotic = **Unrealistic**
O. Redolent = **Evocative**
P. Sclerotic = **Hard**
Q. Supercilious = **Arrogance**

4. In the dance of finance, ~~astute~~ **shrewd** individuals employ a ~~judicious amalgam~~ **careful mix** of research, ~~prudence~~ **caution**, and ~~malleability~~ **flexibility** to ~~navigate~~ **steer** through the intricacies of markets, ensuring their financial ~~endeavors~~ **efforts** are not merely transactions but ~~proficient~~ **skillful** strategies for durable success.

6. Frida Kahlo, the ~~illustrious~~ **famous** Mexican surrealist, transcends ~~mere~~ artistic ~~paradigms~~ **structures**, ~~encapsulating a profound fusion of poignant~~ **fusing** introspection and ~~visceral~~ symbolism within ~~the~~ **her** intricate ~~tapestry of her oeuvre~~ **work**, ~~thereby rendering~~ **establishing** her **as** a ~~luminary provocateur of~~ **radical figure in** avant-garde expression.

Chapter 9

1. Fix the following sentences.
   A. A study found that approximately ~~30%~~ **thirty percent** of participants reported feeling alienated from their community, highlighting the social fragmentation present in modern society.
   B. Among the ~~forty two~~ **forty-two** artifacts uncovered at the excavation site, several showed evidence of early tool-making techniques.
   C. In a study of ~~75~~ **seventy-five** urban neighborhoods, researchers found that social cohesion significantly reduced crime rates.

D. In the ~~1920's~~ **1920s**, the Surrealist movement captivated the art world with its exploration of the unconscious mind and dream imagery.
E. In the ~~twentieth-century~~ **twentieth century**, existentialist philosophers like Jean-Paul Sartre and Simone de Beauvoir explored themes of freedom, choice, and the nature of existence.
F. In ~~twentieth century~~ **twentieth-century** Latin American literature, magical realism emerged as a prominent literary style, blending fantastical elements with realistic narratives.
G. ~~120~~ **One hundred and twenty** developing countries received financial aid to support infrastructure projects.
H. Researchers found that of ~~two hundred and fifty~~ **250** participants, ~~two hundred and twenty five~~ **225** reported experiencing increased anxiety levels during the pandemic.
I. Smith contends that *To the Lighthouse* "is a work of mourning, an attempt to come to terms with loss" (~~Nine~~ **9**).
J. The deforestation rate in the Amazon rainforest has increased by ~~25~~ **twenty-five** percent over the past decade, posing serious environmental challenges.
K. The ~~18th~~ **eighteenth** century was a period of significant political and intellectual change, characterized by the Enlightenment and the American and French Revolutions.

2. Fix the following sentences.
   A. *A Portrait ~~Of The~~ Artist As A Young Man A Portrait **of the** Artist as a Young Man* depicts the development of a young man's artistic consciousness amid the confines of early twentieth-century Ireland.
   B. During the Civil Rights Movement, ~~"Jet"~~ ***Jet*** magazine played a crucial role in shaping public opinion and disseminating news to African American communities across the United States.
   C. In ~~"Anna Karenina,"~~ ***Anna Karenina,*** Leo Tolstoy masterfully weaves together the tragic story of Anna's doomed love affair with profound insights into Russian society and the human psyche.
   D. In ~~*The Lottery*~~ **"The Lottery,"** Shirley Jackson offers a chilling story that unveils the sinister underbelly of a seemingly ordinary small town through its annual ritual.

E. ~~"Hamlet"~~ ***Hamlet*** explores themes of revenge, madness, and the complexity of the human condition.
F. James Baldwin's essay ~~*Down at the Cross*~~ **"Down at the Cross"** powerfully examines the intersections of race, religion, and identity in America.
G. *Love ~~In The~~ Time ~~Of~~ Cholera Love* ***in the*** *Time* ***of*** *Cholera,* by Gabriel García Márquez, portrays love as enduring and transformative, set against the backdrop of a cholera epidemic in a Caribbean town.
H. The ~~"Chicago Tribune"~~ ***Chicago Tribune*** famously printed the premature headline "Dewey Defeats Truman" in its 1948 edition, highlighting the risks of sample bias in election forecasting.
I. *The Sound ~~And The~~ Fury The Sound* ***and the*** *Fury* employs innovative narrative techniques to depict the decline of the Compson family in the post–Civil War South.
J. Thomas Paine's pamphlet ~~"Common Sense"~~ ***Common Sense*** was instrumental in swaying public opinion in favor of American independence from British rule.
K. Through the metaphor of two diverging paths in a forest, ~~*The Road Not Taken*~~ **"The Road Not Taken"** explores the theme of choices and their implications.

3. Fix the following sentences.
   A. In the iconic opening words of *Moby Dick* the narrator ~~declared~~ **declares**, "Call me Ishmael."
   B. The opening lines of *Moby Dick* prepare the reader for the contemplative and philosophical novel to come. **Melville writes:** "Some years ago—never mind how long precisely—having little or no money in my purse, and nothing particular to interest me on shore, I thought I would sail about a little and see the watery part of the world."
   C. Ishmael grimly declares**,** "This is my substitute for pistol and ball."
   D. Ishmael justifies his going to sea by declaring **that,** "It is a way I have of driving off the spleen and regulating circulation."
   E. Note how casually Ishmael speaks of going to **sea,:** "Some years ago—never mind how long precisely—having little or no money in my purse, and nothing particular to interest

me on shore, I thought I would sail about a little and see the watery part of the world."

F. "Some years ago—never mind how long precisely—having little or no money in my purse and nothing particular to interest me on **shore,"**~~,"~~ Ishmael recounts, "I thought I would sail about a little and see the watery part of the world".

G. Speaking of how going to sea fends off thoughts of suicide, Ishmael observes, "This is my substitute for ball and pistol~~." (1)~~**" (1).**

H. In a long passage in the opening paragraph of the novel, Ishmael describes why he has chosen to go to sea:

> ~~"~~Call me Ishmael. Some years ago—never mind how long precisely—having little or no money in my purse, and nothing particular to interest me on shore, I thought I would sail about a little and see the watery part of the world. It is a way I have of driving off the spleen and regulating the circulation.~~"~~ (1)

I. In a long passage in the opening paragraph of the novel, Ishmael confesses how going to sea saves him from what today we would call depression:

> Whenever I find myself growing grim about the mouth; whenever it is a damp, drizzly November in my soul; whenever I find myself involuntarily pausing before coffin warehouses, and bringing up the rear of every funeral I meet; and especially whenever my hypos get such an upper hand of me, that it requires a strong moral principle to prevent me from deliberately stepping into the street, and methodically knocking people's hats off—then, I account it high time to get to sea as soon as I can. (1)

For Ishmael, the sea represents a reprieve from the land. **[Do not indent after block quote.]**

J. By way of introducing himself, Ishmael reports that "Whenever I find myself growing grim about the **mouth... then** I account it high time to get to sea as soon as I can" (1).

Answers to Quizzes

1. In ~~**"Macbeth"**~~ ***Macbeth***~~,~~ guilt pervades the narrative and drives the characters to commit heinous acts. Guilt in the play manifests in three main ways: hallucinations and visions, physical manifestations like sleepwalking, and ~~**how the mental states of its characters slowly deteriorate**~~ **the deteriorating mental states of characters.** Lady Macbeth descends into madness ~~**due to the fact that**~~ **because** she cannot escape the overwhelming guilt stemming from Duncan's murder. **Tortured by guilt,** ~~**the sleepwalking scene**~~ **she sleepwalks, which** vividly portrays her inner turmoil. Her guilt drives her to madness~~, proving that~~ ~~**"what goes around comes around."**~~**. Because she cannot escape her guilt~~.~~, she cannot live.**

   Macbeth's guilt is exacerbated by his ~~**past**~~ **history** of ambition, ruthlessness, and relentless pursuit of power. ~~The murder of King Duncan~~ ~~**is regretted by Macbeth**~~. **Macbeth regrets murdering King Duncan.** Harassed by his conscience, Macbeth confesses **that**~~,~~ "full of scorpions is my ~~**mind. (2. 2)"**~~ **mind" (2.2).**

   Both Macbeth and Lady Macbeth are consumed by **remorse** ~~**and regret**~~ for their treacherous deed. **This remorse** weighs heavily on their minds and souls, driving them to madness and despair~~,~~**;** **it** is a stark reminder of the consequences unchecked ambition and moral transgression can have. The characters are tormented by ~~**an ineffable sense of peccability**~~ **indescribable sense of human sinfulness,** as they ~~**encounter the irrevocable moral transgressions**~~ **face the crimes that cannot be taken back and** that ~~**besiege**~~ **haunt** their every waking moment.

2. Reading through social media posts, **people feel like** time flies by. Social media has transformed how people consume news, connect with others, and ~~accessing~~ **access** entertainment. **Social media** ~~Profoundly impacting~~ **profoundly impacts** society in both positive and negative ways.

   Social media platforms offer users a variety of features, including messaging, photo sharing**,** and live streaming. It allows people to connect and communicate with others, even when they are not in ~~close~~ proximity. Social media offers an endless ~~and infinite~~ array of content. Its platforms have ~~catalyzed a paradigm shift in~~ **changed** interpersonal communication, ~~fostering unprecedented levels of interconnectivity and information dissemination~~ **connecting people and spreading information like never before.**

   Social media undoubtedly creates these opportunities~~,~~**;** however, excessive use can cause feelings of isolation and anxiety, especially among young women. Social media amplifies their insecurities, leading to increased rates of anxiety and depression. On social media, a well-crafted image can often convey a message more effectively than a lengthy post~~, truly exemplifying the adage a picture is worth a thousand words~~. ~~This~~ **These images** can lead to a distorted perception of reality, contributing to poor self-esteem and body image issues. As Donna Jackson Nakazawa explains in *Girls* ~~*On The*~~ ***on the*** *Brink*, “The signs are everywhere: girls are struggling, their mental well-being in ~~decline (tk)”.~~ **decline” (tk).**

   ~~More regulation of social media is deemed necessary by many.~~ **Many call for more regulation of social media.** ~~In the event that~~ **If** social media usage continues to rise unchecked, its effect on mental health could become increasingly concerning.

3. Redlining was a discriminatory practice used by banks, companies**,** and other financial institutions to deny or limit mortgage loans or insurance to certain neighborhoods based on their racial or ethnic composition. The term originated from the practice of lenders drawing red lines on maps to delineate areas where they would not invest~~,~~**.** ~~these~~ **These** areas were often characterized by high concentrations of minority residents, particularly African Americans and Latinos. In the ~~1930’s~~ **1930s**, the Home Owners’

Loan Corporation (HOLC) redlined around ~~85~~ **eighty-five** neighborhoods in Chicago.

Redlining practices were unfair ~~and unjust~~, as they systematically favored certain racial groups while discriminating against others. Redlining led to inequalities across the board: in restricted access to housing; in limited educational opportunities; and ~~it~~ **in** diminished economic prospects for many communities. The ~~end~~ result was the creation of segregated neighborhoods, with lasting effects on community development and wealth accumulation.

Even though redlining led to disparities in wealth, housing, and opportunity~~.~~**, it persisted for decades.** ~~Redlining was criticized by activists~~ **Activists criticized redlining** for perpetuating systemic discrimination in housing markets. Determined to address the issue, ~~the practice was swiftly condemned by~~ the committee devoted to drawing up the Fair Housing Act of 1968 **swiftly condemned the practice.**

~~In spite of the fact that~~ **Although** redlining was officially banned in the 1960s, its legacy continues to affect communities of color in any number of ways. This **legacy** is evident in the unequal distribution of resources, which perpetuated a cycle of disadvantage for marginalized communities. Despite efforts to ~~ameliorate~~ **undo** its ~~impacts~~ **effects**, redlining ~~entrenched systemic~~ **sealed in** inequities and ~~exacerbated socioeconomic~~ **worsened** disparities for generations. Banks and lending institutions promised equal opportunity, but actions speak louder than words. [**Here is an instance when you might leave the cliché.**]

Notes

Chapter 2

1. The classic example comes from the Iran-Contra affair. In the 1980s, the United States sold arms to Iran and used the proceeds to buy arms for the anti-communist Contras in Nicaragua. Congress had forbidden both actions. When the affair came to light in 1987, Ronald Reagan, in a State of the Union address, admitted that "serious mistakes were made." He did not specify *by whom* the serious mistakes were made. The answer was his administration. And one could argue whether they were in fact mistakes since they seem to have been done quite deliberately. Note, however, that other presidents (Bill Clinton, George W. Bush) would also take advantage of the weaselly omission the passive voice allows.

2. Bryan A. Garner, *Garner's Modern English Usage* (New York: Oxford, 2022), 807.

3. William Strunk, Jr. and E. B. White, *The Elements of Style* (Boston: Allyn and Bacon, 2000), 18.

4. Stephen Pinker, *The Sense of Style* (New York: Penguin, 2014), 55.

5. You should avoid, however, toggling between the tornado and the town as subjects. Doing so can leave readers feeling dizzy: "The tornado leveled the town. Its shopping mall was razed to the ground. The tornado went on to destroy the fireworks factory. The historical district is ruined beyond repair."

6. It comes in my paragraph on sentences as stories. "The acted upon (the town) is promoted to the subject, while the actor (the tornado) is shuffled off to the end of the sentence." Neither clause has an actor: who or what promotes the acted upon or who or what shuffles the actor off to the end of the sentence. I could have written the sentence in the active voice: "*The writer* promotes the acted upon (the town) to the subject and shuffles the tornado off to the end of the sentence." But this sentence is not about writers. It is about passive-voice sentences and what happens to the acted upon and the actor in them. The passive voice is therefore appropriate.

Chapter 3

1. Bill Martin Jr. and Eric Carle, *Brown Bear, Brown Bear, What Do You See?* (New York: Henry Holt, 1996).

2. *Whom* if the direct object is a person: *She painted the child.* Whom did she paint? *The child.* Note that I speak here of direct objects. Indirect objects are nouns or pronouns that receive the direct object. In the sentence *The baker gave the woman a cake,* the direct object is *the cake*—it is what is given—and the indirect object is *the woman,* the noun or pronoun to whom the cake is given.

3. Richard A. Lanham, *Revising Prose* (New York: Pearson Longman, 2007), 12.

Chapter 4

1. I borrow this observation from Richard Bullock, Michael Brody, and Francine Weinberg, *The Little Seagull Handbook* (New York: Norton, 2022), 378–379.

Chapter 5

1. Benjamin Dreyer, *Dreyer's English* (New York: Random House, 2019), 254.

2. H. W. Fowler, *A Dictionary of Modern English Usage,* 2nd edition (Oxford: Oxford University Press, 1926), 91. Note that Fowler lived in less sensitive times than we do. Today, few would write "handicapped" so casually. Note, too, that men can also wear bonnets. Picture what a Scotsman playing the bagpipes wears atop his head. That is also a bonnet.

3. Richard Bullock, Michael Brody, and Francine Weinberg, *The Little Seagull Handbook* (New York: Norton, 2022), 386.

Chapter 6

1. C. Rexford Davis, *Toward Correct English I* (1936), quoted in Bryan A. Garner, *Garner's Modern English Usage* (New York: Oxford, 2022), 587. I have changed "predicate" to "verb." These terms differ, but verb is the more familiar term and sufficient for this chapter.

2. Granted, "Reflecting on the nature of existence" could function as a subject: *Reflecting on the nature of existence is how philosophers spend their time.*

3. The Oxford comma supposedly earned its name because editors at Oxford University Press insisted writers use it. No one has summoned any evidence for this claim, but the supposition has circulated so widely and for so long that the name has stuck. Because it refers to its purpose, the serial comma is probably a better term.

4. I borrow these examples from Bryan A. Garner, *Garner's Modern English Usage* (New York: Oxford, 2022), 984.

5. Actually, they substituted semicolons for commas and changed "distribution of" to "distributing of" to make the activity parallel to the other activities. See chapter four for a discussion of parallelism. Daniel Victor, "Oxford Comma Dispute Is Settled as Maine Drivers Get $5 Million," *New York Times*, Feb. 9, 2018, https://www.nytimes.com/2018/02/09/us/oxford-comma-maine.html

6. Benjamin Dreyer, *Dreyer's English* (New York: Random House, 2019), 24.

Chapter 8

1. William Strunk Jr. and E. B. White, *The Elements of Style* (Boston: Allyn and Bacon, 2000), 76–77.

2. The other source feeding English is Greek, which, in addition to Anglo-Saxon and Norman French, made its way into the language at various times over the last two thousand years. Thanks to it, English has words like democracy, philosophy, telephone, biology, and history. Greek-to-English words tend not to sound as pompous as Latin-to-English words.

3. Even the term "pretentious diction" sails in from other shores. *Pretentious* is a later borrowing from the French. *Diction* arrives with the Normans. It derives from the Latin verb *dicere*: to say.

4. Steven Marche, "Everybody Is Talking About A.I. What the Heck Is It, Anyway?" *New York Times*, January 31, 2024. https://www.nytimes.com/2024/01/31/books/review/artificial-intelligence-best-books.html

5. Jesse Wegman, "Trump's Immunity Case Was Settled More Than 200 Years Ago." *New York Times*, April 26, 2024. https://www.nytimes.com/2024/04/26/opinion/trump-immunity-founding-fathers.html

Chapter 9

1. Toni Morrison, *Beloved* (New York: Vintage, [1989] 2019).

2. Herman Melville, *Moby Dick* (New York: Penguin, [1851] 2003).

3. Frederick Douglass, *Narrative of the Life of Frederick Douglass, an American Slave* (New York: Penguin, [1845] 2014).

Chapter 10

1. H. W. Fowler, *A Dictionary of Modern English Usage*, 2nd edition (Oxford: Oxford University Press, 1926), 635.

2. Ursula K. Le Guin, *Steering the Craft* (Boston: Houghlin Mifflin, 2015), 17.

3. Rosina Lippi-Green, *English with an Accent: Language, Ideology, and Discrimination in the United States* (New York: Routledge, 2012), 67.

4. April Baker-Bell, *Linguistic Justice: Black Language, Literacy, Identity, and Pedagogy* (New York: Routledge, 2020), 11.

5. Baker-Bell, *Linguistic Justice*, 24.

6. Vershawn Ashanti Young, "Should Writers Use They Own English?" *Iowa Journal of Cultural Studies* 12, no. 1 (2010), 110–117.

7. It goes without saying that the same advice would apply to any group whose English departs from White Mainstream English. Regardless, if AI further associates writing with White Mainstream English, that will make it all the harder to recognize other dialects as equals.